Anthea Dove lives with her  Yorkshire. After retiring from a member of the ecumenical Suffolk. She has written nine (quiet days, and has a strong co ......ng for social justice and ecumenism.

FOR THE LOVE OF GOD

Meditations for Christian Living

ANTHEA DOVE

First published in Great Britain in 2007

Society for Promoting Christian Knowledge
36 Causton Street
London SW1P 4ST

British Library Cataloguing-in-Publication Data
A catalogue record for this book is available from the British Library

ISBN 978–0–281–05838–9

1 3 5 7 9 10 8 6 4 2

Typeset by Graphicraft Ltd, Hong Kong
Printed in Great Britain by Bookmarque Ltd, Croydon, Surrey

To Brother Mole
with affection and gratitude

Contents

Preface

The title of this book is deliberately ambiguous. This is because while some of the meditations are focused on God's amazing, unconditional love for us, the greater part of them are concerned with *our* love for *him*, which can be expressed in many and various ways. If we try to walk with God, we can find him not only in places and things, but also in people and situations. He/she touches our lives, not only through the working of the Holy Spirit, but through the power of the human spirit too.

These reflections are a response to Scripture and lead us in different directions: to worship and praise or into relationship with others. The Bible inspires us over and over again as we listen to God's word, and the meditations flow from that source. In the Roman Catholic Church in the 1960s, a council was held known popularly as Vatican II, and a document from that council, *Dei Verbum* (The Word of God) states:

> In the sacred books, the Father who is in heaven,
> comes lovingly to meet his children and to talk to
> them.

So God comes lovingly to meet those who read this book and respond to his word in different ways: with wonder, with a renewal of faith, perhaps, and a deeper understanding, with greater commitment and, indeed, with questioning.

The meditations are intended to be reflected upon slowly; one day at a time may suffice. But however we respond, we can be sure that God is with us as we read.

Acknowledgements

I would like to thank Alison Barr for her thoughtful, careful editing of this book.

God's dwelling

How lovely is your dwelling place,
O LORD of hosts!

Psalm 84.1

When I listen to this beautiful psalm, my mind immediately leaps to certain places: to Durham Cathedral or York Minster where the great age and gracefulness of the soaring arches and the dazzling beauty of the stained glass seem to speak of the presence of God. Then I think of the small chapel of the Little Sisters of Jesus at Walsingham: simple and plain and beautiful: and, one might say, 'full of God'. I remember the Friends' Meeting House in my town: simple and plain but hardly beautiful, yet surely God is there too.

And after all, the Holy Spirit is not confined to buildings. We find her in all sorts of places: perhaps in the mountains, by the sea, in a quiet garden or a busy street. Some of us may find her in hospital or prison. God makes her dwelling place among her people, within their hearts, within their attitudes and actions. She is to be found wherever there is love, wherever there is suffering and most especially where human, holy love reaches out with compassion.

> Where is God?
> Where is her dwelling place?
> She dwells wherever there is beauty,
> wherever there is kindness,
> wherever there is pain.
> She dwells in the hearts of the brave,
> in the souls of the dying,
> in every act of tenderness.
> Her dwelling place is lovely
> beyond our understanding.

* * *

1

Old age

The glory of youths is their strength,
but the beauty of the aged is their grey hair.

Proverbs 20.29

As I think about my age, I am not especially cheered by this proverb!

I can't run up the hill any more; I can't turn cartwheels. There are wrinkles on my face and the colour has faded from my hair. I can't remember the names of flowers or the dates of wars. My memory is feebler, and my body too. The children I bore and suckled and fussed over are grown and gone away. But I don't think that my life is over, or even that I'm on the way downhill.

I believe in wholeness: that mind, body, heart and soul are all interdependent, that when we are under mental stress our bodies suffer. But I also believe that in old age, when the body loses much of its attractiveness and vigour and the mind is slow to remember, there is a new opportunity for the growth of the spirit.

George Herbert wrote: 'All may have, if they dare try, a glorious life,' and 'all' certainly includes the old. I find that whereas I have always been moved by dog roses in the hedges, the tiny perfection of the newly born, the wild winds howling across the moors and the courage of people who have suffered greatly, now I am touched more profoundly by all these things, and every day I seem to find a new source of delight. My sense of wonder grows, my feelings of compassion deepen.

I have time now to pray, and my joy in life springs from the time I spend with God. His Spirit flows into every part of my life, into my relationships. The children I cared for are now my friends. I am learning slowly and painfully to see my own weaknesses more clearly, and trying at the same time to see in others the tears that are not shed and to hear the words that are not spoken.

For me life is beautiful, terrible and exciting, the gift of God which I accept with eager hands and a hopeful heart.

* * *

2

Coming to Jesus 1

He said to them, 'Come and see.'
John 1.39

Jesus said to him, 'If you wish to be perfect, go, sell your possessions and give the money to the poor, and you will have treasure in heaven; then come, follow me.'

Matthew 19.21

Come to me, all you that are weary and are carrying heavy burdens, and I will give you rest.

Matthew 11.28

Jesus seems to have used the word 'come' often. When two of John's disciples, following him out of curiosity, asked 'Where are you staying?' he said to them, 'Come and see.' It was an invitation. He also invited the rich young man who wanted to attain eternal life, to come and follow him. And he reaches out in welcome to all of us who are overburdened, struggling, exhausted or stressed, offering us the rest and peace we need.

The simple word 'come' is a word of welcome. On the lips of Jesus it draws us in from the cold, from loneliness, from a misguided way of living. When he uses this word he is expressing the all-embracing welcome our God has for each one of us, and his invitation to a new way of being. When Jesus says, 'Come!' we do not need to spring to attention, ready to obey; rather, we fall into the arms of God as the prodigal son fell into the arms of his father.

* * *

Coming to Jesus 2

You said, 'Come!'
but I wasn't listening.
I was enjoying myself.

You said, 'Come!'
But I was too busy

3

being a wife, a mother,
a neighbour and a friend.

You said, 'Come!'
But I drew back,
beginning to realize
a little of what it would mean.

You said, 'Come!'
and I needed you
but didn't dare.
I thought I was unworthy.

Today, in the silence,
I hear you say, 'Come!'
I am afraid to lose
my dependence on human love,
but I stretch my hand towards you,
knowing you will meet me
more than half way.

So soon I will come to you,
And I will follow
And see where you live.

And then I shall be free
To love truly.

* * *

Beauty and sadness

I lift up my eyes to the hills . . .
Psalm 121.1

It's hard not to envy my friend Alison. From every window in her house she can lift up her eyes to the hills, but from my house there are none to be seen. At least, unlike many people, I live on the edge of hilly country, and one reason I love to go walking there is that I like to stand still and lift up my eyes to the

4

high horizon. In the silence and majesty of the hills I sense the presence of God and his glory.

Not long ago, I went walking in some hills where there used to be lead-mining. At first, the walk was delightful. We climbed a rocky path above a beck and through ancient woodland where primroses, violets and bluebells were flourishing. But when we left the wood the weather changed, the skies grew dark and the landscape was eerily bleak. We began to climb steeply and suddenly came upon a scene of utter desolation, black abandoned mine workings making a menacing silhouette on the summit ahead.

As the rain began to seep through my so-called waterproof, I thought of the thousands of miners who had passed this way, weary and under-nourished, risking their health and their lives, never sure of being paid for their miserable, dangerous toil. I wondered if in spring any of them lifted their eyes to marvel at the patch of bluebells on the hillside opposite. I wondered: if you have an empty belly, an aching back and several miles to trudge home to where your hungry children wait in hope, do you care about bluebells? Perhaps . . . ?

The next day was bright and clear. We set off to climb again.

* * *

Faithfulness

When they had entered the city, they went to the room upstairs where they were staying, Peter and John, and James, and Andrew, Philip and Thomas, Bartholomew and Matthew, James son of Alphaeus and Simon the Zealot, and Judas son of James. All these were constantly devoting themselves to prayer, together with certain women, including Mary the mother of Jesus.

Acts 1.13–14

When I read about these apostles in the early days before the coming of the Holy Spirit, and their transformation, I feel humbled to think of their faithfulness, prayerfulness and courage. The day after our walk among the lead mines, we took a different path, using a guide book. The instructions advised us to turn off the main path and climb up a narrow cleft in the hills, Swinnergill, to where, towards the end of the seventeenth century, a group of dissenters used to meet together for worship, in secret for fear of persecution.

This sounded intriguing, so we started up the near-vertical route. It led us high above a beck which was rollicking over rocks below, and as someone with a fear of heights I found the very narrow slippery path challenging. I kept thinking about any women among those long-ago dissenters, who surely were not equipped with proper climbing boots.

I had expected to find the cave, which is known as Swinner's Kirk, after about ten minutes, but we had spent over an hour slithering down to the beck, struggling to cross where there was neither footbridge nor stepping stones, scrambling on all fours up the other side of the gill, before it became too dangerous to go any further. So we never reached the dissenters' cave. I thought of them and wondered at their courage and fortitude, at the strength of their faith which made them undertake such a difficult journey in order to worship God together. Just as the previous day I had felt humbled to think of the brave lead miners, so in Swinnergill I felt full of admiration for the brave dissenters. And I thought how our God, ever present in the magnificent hills, is also constantly at work in the human spirit.

* * *

Alone 1

I do nothing on my own, but I speak these things as the Father instructed me. And the one who sent me is with me: he has not left me alone.

John 8.28–29

These few words give us a glimpse into the humanity of Jesus. It shows his dependence on his Father and implies that he would be lonely without God's constant presence.

It is interesting that throughout both Old and New Testaments there is scarcely any mention of loneliness. There are frequent references to the plight of the poor, the sick, strangers and those in prison. All of these were pressing issues requiring justice and mercy, yet the lonely are not included in the list of those who are in need of compassion and fair treatment.

But for those who live in our present-day western world, loneliness is a terrible scourge, the cause of widespread, often hidden distress. How is it that there was far less loneliness in biblical times and that it is rare, even now, in developing countries?

In the west old people generally dread becoming a burden on their children, and very often the children live far away. The streets of back-to-back housing in our cities were usually dreary and cramped, with inadequate sanitation, but each street was a community with neighbours looking out for one another, so only someone with a difficult temperament, arrogant or hot-tempered perhaps, was likely to be lonely.

I think we all need to recognize the potential of community, wherever we live, and even more importantly we can make the effort to seek out those who feel abandoned and depressingly alone.

* * *

Alone 2

I'm sorry, of course I am.
I wouldn't want anyone close to me
to take her own life.
But of course that's part of the trouble,
she wasn't close to anyone.
I didn't even know her name.
She didn't seem at all friendly,

in fact I don't think I ever saw her smile.
She wasn't what you would call a joiner,
if you know what I mean.
She wouldn't join the Women's Institute
or the sewing circle that meets on Tuesdays.
I heard the vicar invited her to come to church
but she didn't turn up.
I would have spoken to her if she had.
The next thing I knew,
the police had broken in and found her.
I'm sorry, like I said,
I still don't know her name,
or why she did it.
She can't have been lonely,
can she?

* * *

Inclusiveness

*And I, when I am lifted up from the earth, will draw all
people to myself.*

John 12.32

What strikes me most about this saying of Jesus is the word 'draw'.
We who are his followers often feel driven – driven to be good,
driven to *do* good – but it is not the way of our God to com-
pel or force us in any direction. Rather, by getting to know him
through the Gospels, we are attracted to him and to his way of
living. But Jesus is not drawing only Christians to himself; he
is drawing *all* people; his love is inclusive, for everyone.

Recently it has become fashionable to present television
programmes in which a group of people are exposed to public
scrutiny and one by one voted off the show by the fellow
members of the group or sometimes by the television audience.
This is the very opposite of inclusiveness; it is taking delight in

8

the unpopularity of others and telling them they no longer belong. Far from being drawn into community, the contestants, one by one, are driven out – and worst of all, viewers are encouraged to enjoy their discomfiture and shame.

Jean Vanier, who chose to spend his life with severely disabled people, wrote that welcoming is not just something that happens to people who cross the threshold, but an attitude: the constant openness of the heart.

* * *

Extraordinary

As they [Elijah and Elisha] continued walking and talking, a chariot of fire and horses of fire separated the two of them, and Elijah ascended in a whirlwind into heaven. Elisha kept watching and crying out, 'Father, father! The chariots of Israel and its horsemen!' But when he could no longer see him, he grasped his own clothes and tore them in two pieces.

2 Kings 2.11–12

When we have an experience that moves us deeply, we are sometimes at a loss to describe it and so we say, 'It was out of this world', a statement that would have been literally true in Elisha's case.

The expression came into my mind as I stood and looked on a beautiful landscape in North Yorkshire lit by the low winter sun. The peace and loveliness of the scene were beyond expression, beyond description.

Such experiences don't happen every day, but when they do we seem to be lifted out of ourselves in ecstasy. It can happen when a sexual encounter is charged with love; it can happen when we listen to music that somehow raises us beyond our ordinary way of being. And yet, the most moving experiences of all often take place in the heart of the market place. Sometimes where there is sin, degradation, despair, one person can break through to another in love in such a way that for a moment the kingdom comes, or, as the hymn tells us, 'Our God reigns'. By this, a life can be transformed.

It is a moment when everything is surrendered to the Holy Spirit who is 'out of this world' and yet everywhere that men and women breathe. And our God, who is at the heart of all that is beautiful and wonderful, is also there in the exchange of love between human beings, in the place where suffering is met with compassion.

* * *

Walking with God

Enoch walked with God; then he was no more, because God took him.

Genesis 5.24

At first sight we know next to nothing about Enoch. He is just a name in a list of the genealogy of the patriarchs who lived before the flood. He was the son of Jared and the father of Methuselah, but this doesn't enlighten us much because we know nothing of them, either, except that Methuselah, dying, we are told, at the age of 969 years, was the longest living of all these venerable patriarchs.

However, Enoch is interesting because he differs in one respect from all the rest of the line. The others simply died, but Enoch was carried off by God much as Elijah was, and for this reason he was given a prominent place in Jewish tradition, where he is seen as a model of holiness.

What draws me to Enoch is none of this, but the statement that he walked with God. This short phrase stands out from the page for me, conjuring up as it does a beautiful image of God and Enoch walking together in perfect harmony and understanding. It also makes me ask: could I walk with God? What does it mean, to walk with God?

10

Ideally, I would like to go somewhere peaceful and beautiful, and above all away from noise and other people. Then I would walk along, imagining God's hand in mine, listening to him, praising him, filled with delighted incredulity to be in his presence.

In the real world, and surrounded by the familiar clutter of my kitchen, I, and anyone else who so wishes, can close my eyes and ask God to be with me and stay with me as I give my time solely to him. In other words, 'walking with God' is a way of describing prayer.

And there is another way of taking this walk: as we go about our ordinary tasks – washing up, cooking, looking after the children, doing our job – as far as possible, to practise the presence of God as the seventeenth-century monk Brother Lawrence advised, keeping our minds and hearts continually turned to him wherever we are and whatever we happen to be doing.

* * *

Community

I will place my dwelling in your midst, and I shall not abhor you. And I will walk among you, and will be your God, and you shall be my people. I am the LORD your God who brought you out of the land of Egypt, to be their slaves no more; I have broken the bars of your yoke and made you walk erect.

Leviticus 26.11–13

At the climax of the Catholic Mass, the priest raises the host and says:

This is the Lamb of God
who takes away the sins of the world.
Happy are those who are called to his supper.

11

Then the people reply:

> Lord, I am not worthy to receive you,
> but only say the word and I shall be healed.

It is a solemn and very personal moment when I acknowledge to myself, and to everyone else, that I certainly do not deserve to receive the body of Christ himself, yet I have faith in his unconditional generous welcome, taking me just as I am.

But after I have received the body and blood of Jesus and spent some time thanking him with a full heart, then it's time to remember that holiness is not just about God and me, but about God and *us*, all of us. For we are his people and he is our God. Jesus has given me himself, and now it is my turn to give his love to my community. In a gathering to worship of God's people, there should be no-one who is lonely, because we all belong to one another. We are bound together by cords of love and unity which nothing should break.

* * *

Refugee 1

> *Where you go, I will go;*
> *where you lodge, I will lodge;*
> *your people shall be my people,*
> *and your God my God.*
> *Where you die, I will die –*
> *there will I be buried.*
> Ruth 1.16–17

Ruth stayed with her mother-in-law because she loved her. But Naomi knew how it would be for Ruth: Moab was a completely strange land with a different culture altogether. Ruth would have no roots, no family, no status, but at least she had the love of Naomi.

This story is moving because of the tenderness between these two women, who vie with each other in unselfishness! Ruth is concerned for Naomi, old and bereaved; Naomi is worried that Ruth, who is from Bethlehem, in Judah, will be unhappy in a land which, although it was Judah's nearest neighbour, was nonetheless a foreign country to her.

How many refugees come to our country to be received with officialdom and coldness, and afterwards open hostility, to be called offensive names, have bricks hurled at them, be denied welcome, friendship or enough money to live on?

* * *

Refugee 2

I was fourteen
when my mother dragged me out of bed in the middle
    of the night.
I was bewildered and scared. I said, 'Mother, what's
    happening?
Why are you doing this?' But she only shook her head.
Tears were pouring down her face when she pushed me
    into the van.
She whispered, 'Don't worry, Sip. You'll be safe soon.
You'll like England, but never forget how much I
    love you.'
She gave me a pill and I fell into a deep sleep.
When I woke I was on an aeroplane.
I kept remembering what my mother said.
England. What was it like?
Would the people speak my language? Would they
    welcome me?

They didn't. They didn't speak my language and they
    didn't welcome me.
They shouted at me because I couldn't understand.
Afterwards they led me into a sort of prison where
    everyone looked miserable.

I told someone my name was 'Sipiwe'. She put her arms
round me, and cried.
I cried too; I thought I would never stop crying
and already I knew I hated this England
and it hated me.

* * *

Climate change

He turns rivers into a desert,
springs of water into thirsty ground,
a fruitful land into a salty waste,
because of the wickedness of its inhabitants.

He turns a desert into pools of water,
a parched land into springs of water.
And there he lets the hungry live,
and they establish a town to live in;
they sow fields, and plant vineyards,
and get a fruitful yield.

Psalm 107.33–37

We no longer think of God as a punishing God, but as one whose
Spirit is in everything: in living water and in the desert, in places
where his people go hungry and with those who go out to feed
them.

It is not God who is changing our climate, already causing
death in creatures like polar bears and making the sea rise to
flood our fertile lands. It is we human beings who through
our greed and indifference are bringing disaster and destruction upon the earth. What kind of world are we bequeathing
to our children and our children's children?

Grandad, were you deaf when they told you what
would happen,
when they said the sea would rise and flood the land?
Grandad, were you blind when they showed you all
those pictures

of animals dying and people so afraid?
Grandad, why didn't you stop them?
Didn't you know how it would be for me?
Didn't you march or protest or write to your
    government?
Did you do nothing, Grandad?
Didn't you think of me?

* * *

Loving another

*Beloved, let us love one another, because love is from God;
everyone who loves is born of God and knows God.*

1 John 4.7

The other day I visited a small community of nuns and was
introduced to a very old sister. I had been curious to meet her
for a long time because she was said to be a wonderful eccentric
but cantankerous with it. She came in smiling and greeted me
warmly. As we talked, I realized she was just as interesting and
fascinating as I had been led to believe, but to my surprise she
seemed gentle, sweet-tempered and glowing with happiness.

After an hour, the sister in charge, Sister Agnes, came and
told the old nun it was time for her rest. She shook hands
with me, smiled benignly and hobbled out of the room like an
obedient child.

When she had gone, Sister Agnes smiled at me. 'She's wonderful, isn't she?' she said. 'Did you know that six weeks ago we
thought she was dying?'

'No,' I answered, surprised. 'What happened?'

'Well,' said Sister Agnes, 'she's 85, you know, and she had a
massive heart attack. We rushed her to hospital but we thought
there was no hope.' She paused, smiled at me a little shyly, and
went on, 'I sat with her that night, holding her hand and praying. She was unconscious but she came round in the early hours.
She looked so frail and I was full of pity for her. I thought she

15

would be dead in a few hours, so I simply said to her, "Sister, I love you."

'I'll never forget how she looked at me. Although she was so weak, she was smiling, with tears in her eyes, and she whispered, "I love you too, Agnes."

'Well, of course, to everyone's amazement she's made a complete recovery and you simply wouldn't believe the difference in her, and in me, too. It's as though just exchanging those words has made us free to love and be loved in a way we never thought possible.'

* * *

The bridegroom's friend

He who has the bride is the bridegroom. The friend of the bridegroom, who stands and hears him, rejoices greatly at the bridegroom's voice. For this reason my joy has been fulfilled. He must increase, but I must decrease.

John 3.29–30

So John the Baptist describes his relationship to Jesus.

I used to find the image of the adult John slightly intimidating. He came over as a stark, ascetic creature. Both the idea of his living in the desert (I don't feel particularly relieved to learn that it was probably locust beans and not actual locusts he fed on!) and the thought of his gruesome and barbaric death (his head dripping blood on a plate) discouraged me from wanting to know more about him. It was only later, when I began to read the Gospels more seriously, particularly the passage above, that John became not only real for me but inspiring.

I find that little speech about the bridegroom's friend a wonderful example of humility. There is no envy or jealousy in John, but the generosity to be truly happy in someone else's happiness. For me it is not easy to be selfless and humble in this way; I enjoy success and praise for myself. But I have seen the lovely qualities of John the Baptist in others. And I have seen the joy on the face of a nun holding her sister's baby in her arms, and the happiness in the smile of a young boy for the success of his friend who had just beaten him in a race.

I would like to be among those who are glad to diminish, so that Christ may increase in me.

* * *

Patience 1

O God, you are my God, I seek you,
my soul thirsts for you;
my flesh faints for you,
as in a dry and weary land
where there is no water.

Psalm 63.1

Sometimes – indeed, quite often – those of us who try to pray find ourselves in an arid place. Although we have set apart a time and a place where we can be still, silent and alone, listening attentively, somehow we fail to find the presence of God. So, we are like a dry, weary land without water and, like the desperately hungry people in some countries who long for the rains, all we can do is wait. What we need is patience, perhaps an underrated virtue.

At such times my greatest consolation lies in remembering that I am a child of God, that my name is written on the palm of his hand, that he has counted every hair of my head. In other words, regardless of what I feel or cannot feel, he has a constant, tender care for me.

We need patience, and our God is himself infinitely patient. He will never give up on us.

* * *

Patience 2

How patient our God is!
I see him as a candle,

waiting for someone to light the flame.
I see him as a tiny seed,
buried deep in the ground,
waiting for the sunshine and the rain,
I see him as a tight bud,
waiting to unfold.
I know him, waiting within me,
waiting for me to grow, to bloom,
to shine, to blaze.

How patient he is,
watching and waiting,
seeing me searching, stumbling, sinning,
seeing my folly and my defiance,
knowing that I long for his truth and beauty
but settle instead for my comfort.

How long, O Lord, will you wait for me?
How can I hesitate to run into your arms,
to abandon everything
that is not of you?
How can I focus, except on you,
who wait so patiently for me?

* * *

Reverence

Now there was a woman who had been suffering from haemorrhages for twelve years; and though she had spent all she had on physicians, no one could cure her. She came up behind [Jesus] and touched the fringe of his clothes, and immediately her haemorrhage stopped.

Luke 8.43–44

This poor woman was too afraid to face Jesus or to speak to him, but her need was so desperate that she did manage to bring herself to touch the fringe of his cloak. Her faith gave her the courage to make this gesture, to reach towards the humanity of Jesus.

She was faced with the same tension that we are still faced with today: as God is great and wonderful beyond our imagining, how can we relate to him (or her) as our brother (or sister)? Is the God who made the universe really pleased to make his home in me? I think the answer must be to ask him! We can share our questions and confusions with him; in other words we can bring such concerns to him in prayer. Best of all, we can continually praise him for the marvels of his creation, and constantly thank him for being our dearest friend.

Sometimes we can distort the idea of reverence for God to absurd lengths. I remember with regret how strict I was with my children when we took them to church. The four little ones were not allowed to turn round, to whisper, to fidget in any way, for a whole hour. That's pretty tough when you are two, three, four and five years old! More importantly, it's hardly conducive to enthusiasm for churchgoing. Now that I am older and perhaps a little wiser, I believe that God wants little children to be happy, in church and everywhere else. I think we can only achieve true reverence when we learn to look at ourselves with genuine humility.

* * *

Risk 1

Now the LORD said to Abram, 'Go from your country and your kindred and your father's house to the land that I will show you.'

Genesis 12.1

I have a friend who is a very peaceable man. He is a hermit, and I go to visit him once every year. He is always gentle and self-effacing. Last time I saw him, as I was waving goodbye I called, 'Take care!' and to my surprise he answered, 'No! Don't say, "Take care," say, "Take risks!"'

Abram took a huge risk. In response to God he left his past behind and set off for a land that was completely unknown. Even today, with all our advances in technology, it takes great courage for someone to leave behind everything familiar and go to settle in a country about which he or she knows nothing.

Missionaries and explorers have of course always been risk-takers, motivated by their love of God and a wish to share their faith, or in search of achievement and perhaps glory. But most of us are too timid and cautious for risk-taking. We would rather be safe than sorry. At one level we might decide not to go to a really interesting film because very heavy rain is forecast, at another we might not be brave enough to introduce ourselves to someone we like the look of in case they dislike us, or we may be too afraid to volunteer to do a night stint at the shelter for the homeless.

At my age I find it extra-tempting to be unadventurous. I can eat what I like when I like. My house is warm and comfortable and full of things that I find beautiful; I have a circle of dear, familiar friends. So why do anything to threaten this happy state of affairs?

I think the answer is that I can't stay cosseted in my cosy little world – not, that is, if I love God – because there are a whole lot of my sisters and brothers out there who don't even know what it is to be cosy. If I am prepared to take risks I can sometimes do something to help them.

* * *

Risk 2

Risk usually takes a certain amount of courage and self-sacrifice. My young friend Helen is an outstanding risk-taker. She used to work as a shepherd in a remote Scottish glen. This was a job she enjoyed, and she loved the wild scenery, the moors and the fast-flowing burns. In the villages around she had many good friends.

However, Helen felt drawn to do something more challenging and of use to suffering humanity, so she applied to work with the Quaker Peace Service, which gave her work in South Africa with children who have been sexually abused and/or have AIDS/HIV. It turned out to be a tough assignment and at times very distressing. Helen worked alone and was often in danger. She had to learn the language from scratch, but it took her no time at all to love the children she tried to help. Helen is young and I am not, but I know I wouldn't have had the courage to take the risks she did at any age.

So, if I'm to take my hermit friend's advice, what should I do now? I can risk the tedium of writing continually to my MP about matters of social justice, I can join in campaigns and marches and demonstrations which might be uncomfortable and exhausting, I can risk people's disapproval by challenging those ideas which I believe to be wrong. However inconvenient it may be, I can visit the sick and housebound and those in prison, and I can give a warm welcome to strangers. And if I am going to take risks I can't do it alone; I need the Holy Spirit to guide and inspire me.

* * *

Beautiful names

> *For a child has been born for us,*
> *a son given to us;*
> *authority rests upon his shoulders;*
> *and he is named*
> *Wonderful Counsellor, Mighty God,*
> *Everlasting Father, Prince of Peace.*
> Isaiah 9.6

In the early twentieth century, the Christian missionary C. F. Andrews went out to India. There he made friends with a Sufi scholar, who said to him, 'You tell me your beautiful names for God and I'll tell you mine.'

When I heard this story, I asked myself what beautiful names I use for God. I call him Loving Compassionate Father rather than Almighty God, because sometimes, as when there are terrible disasters or when, in spite of all my pleas, my child died, God certainly does not seem all-powerful. At such times, the name Emmanuel, meaning 'God with us', is more appropriate, since I believe him to be present and close with all who suffer.

As for Jesus, he deserves the titles Saviour and Redeemer, but most often I think of him as Brother and Friend. When I sit in meditation with a lit candle in front of me, I bow to him as Light of the World.

The Holy Spirit is my Comforter and Encourager, the one who puts new heart in me and gives me inspiration. She is the Source of Love and Truth, and of any good that I might do.

This is a very personal list and includes only a few of the ways I relate to my God. Each believer, whether Christian, Sufi, Hindu, Jewish, Zoroastrian or devotee of any religion, will have his or her own list of 'beautiful names' as Isaiah did.

* * *

The Big Issue *seller's mite*

He looked up and saw rich people putting their gifts into the treasury; he also saw a poor widow put in two small copper coins. He said, 'Truly, I tell you, this poor widow has put in more than all of them; for all of them have contributed out of their abundance, but she out of her poverty has put in all she had to live on.'

Luke 21.1–4

Whenever I hear this story I feel ashamed. I do give money to different charities, but I keep back enough to live in comfort and enjoy myself.

There are, however, some people who are far more generous than me. Charlie is one of them, the homeless man who used to sell the *Big Issue* directly across the street from my friend Wendy's office. Over the years the office workers got to know Charlie, and Wendy managed to wheedle out of him the date of his birthday.

When the day came round, Wendy gave Charlie a box of chocolates. He burst into tears, telling her it was the first birthday present he had received in years. Of course, Wendy went back and told the other office workers what Charlie had said. Some time later, Roger, one of Wendy's colleagues, went over to Charlie and gave him two cinema tickets.

Charlie decided it was too much. He didn't need to go to the cinema, so when he saw a young single mother he knew approaching with her child in a buggy, he gave her the tickets. 'Find a babysitter, love,' he said, 'and find somebody to go with you. It's time you went and enjoyed yourself.'

The *Big Issue* seller was like the widow who gave her mite. I ask myself how much I am like either of them.

* * *

The shepherd

He is like a shepherd feeding his flock,
gathering lambs in his arms,
holding them against his breast
and leading to their rest the mother ewes.
     Isaiah 40.11, New Jerusalem Bible

I myself shall pasture my sheep, I myself shall give them rest,
declares the Lord Yahweh. I shall look for the lost one, bring
back the stray, bandage the wounded and make the sick strong.
I shall watch over the fat and healthy.
     Ezekiel 34.15–16, New Jerusalem Bible

In different parts of the Bible, we find evidence of God's amazing, extravagant love for you and me. It is wonderful to know that God loves us so much. The picture of God holding the lambs (that is, us) close to his breast is deeply moving. But for me, the image in Ezekiel, also of sheep, is even more powerful. God doesn't just pour his generous love on nice people, good people, religious people, but equally he pours it on those who have for one reason or another abandoned their faith in him, and those who have never known him. This is what unconditional love means. God loves us just as we are.

I am writing this on Christmas Eve. A young friend is staying with us who has a history of drugs and prison. We invited him to come to Midnight Mass with us and he is trying to come to a decision about this. It is not easy for the 'lost and strayed' to return to the fold.

> Can a woman forget her baby at her breast,
> feel no pity for the child she has borne?
> Even if these were to forget,
> I shall not forget you.
> Look, I have engraved you on the palms of my hands.
> Isaiah 49.15, New Jerusalem Bible

* * *

Total generosity 1

Now Jesus was in one of the towns when a man appeared, covered with leprosy. Seeing Jesus, he fell on his face and implored him. 'Sir,' he said, 'if you want to, you can cure me.' Jesus stretched out his hand, touched him and said, 'Of course I want to! Be cured!' and the leprosy left him at once.
Luke 5.12–13, Jerusalem Bible

I have always particularly liked this story. When I hear it read I think of the leper as being at one with all those who are, and have been through the ages, the outcasts of society, the ones despised and rejected by the comfortable, complacent majority. In our own day, I think of those driven to seek asylum, those severely disabled in mind or body, the failures, the inadequate, the unloved.

24

I am also struck by the fact that Jesus actually touched the leper, who was not only unclean but infectious. Sometimes a touch can convey more feeling than words. The leper must have been astonished and possibly so overwhelmed with gratitude that he hardly cared any more whether he would be cured or not.

I have often reflected on this passage in this way, yet it was something else that surprised and moved me when I read it recently in the translation of the Jerusalem Bible. How did Jesus respond when the leper boldly said to him, 'If you want to, you can cure me'? Jesus said, 'Of course I want to!' The warmth and fervour in those few words bring him alive for us. He cares, and he cares passionately. That is the sort of person he was. That phrase embodies his attitude to the weak and the needy, to you and me. Of course he wants to.

* * *

Total generosity 2

When eight-year-old Will's mother was seriously ill and taken to hospital, his father decided it would be best if Will went away to stay with his cousin in Yorkshire. Will burst into tears at this news. 'But I don't want to go! I want to stay with you!' he shouted. 'I don't know your cousin. I want to be near Mum. Please don't make me go!'

But his father was adamant. 'I'm sorry, Will, but you'll have to go. There's no-one to look after you here. Besides, you'll find my cousin Dorothy is very nice.'

After a long and miserable journey, the coach arrived in York. Will was near to panic. He hung back, dreading the meeting. He waited till everyone else had climbed down from the coach, then stepped down, keeping his eyes on the ground.

When he forced himself to look up he knew at once that it would be all right. The woman who must be Dorothy was smiling down at him, her arms held wide ready to embrace him as she said, 'Oh, Will, I'm so happy! I'm so glad you've come!'

As the story of Will illustrates, even something as simple as a warm and welcoming smile can reflect that generous love which Jesus conveyed to the leper in this spontaneous response. Most of us, sadly, have a tendency to be cautious or even grudging when others make what we perceive as demands on us, and perhaps this is particularly true of the stereotypical British person, who would much prefer to shake hands than hug. But it isn't words or gestures that matter so much as the disposition of the heart.

* * *

Nutty mother?

When they saw this, they made known what had been told them about this child, and all who heard it were amazed at what the shepherds told them. But Mary treasured all these words and pondered them in her heart.

Luke 2.17–19

I like thinking about Mary. I wonder what kind of mother she was. We imagine her as exceptionally virtuous and holy, but she was also human, and I think she must have done a lot of pondering as she watched Jesus grow up. After all, he was human too. I thought about all this after Joe's surprise attack. 'Why do you have to be different from the 60 million other people in this country?' he began, with considerable bitterness in his voice. Joe is my sixth child and I've grown used to aggression and unfair accusations in adolescence, but I was genuinely thrown by this particular attack.

'I didn't know I was different,' I answered. 'I thought I was pretty ordinary.'

'Oh, come off it, Mum,' countered Joe. 'You're a religious mania!'

'Maniac,' I corrected him automatically. Nobody releasing a pent-up flow of indignation wants his use of English criticized, least of all my unacademic, outraged Joe.

'I said you're a maniac, and you are!' he retorted.

'You're a nutter, Mum. You've got to face it.'

Well, I did face it. I faced the idea that I am a nutter, a maniac; and I came to the conclusion that I am not.

I can see I irritate and perhaps embarrass my son by going to church more than once a week and by not frequenting the pub in my spare time as more admirable parents do. But although I would gladly comply with Joe's wishes if he said, 'Please don't wear that purple hat when you come to school,' I am not prepared to give up my pursuit of holiness or pretend to be other than I am, even for him. He will have to bear bravely the stigma of having a religious nut for a mother.

* * *

Who is the sinner?

Two men went up to the temple to pray, one a Pharisee, the other a tax collector. The Pharisee stood there and said this prayer to himself, 'I thank you, God, that I am not grasping, unjust, adulterous like the rest of mankind, and particularly that I am not like this tax collector here. I fast twice a week, I pay tithes on all I get.' The tax collector stood some distance away, not daring even to raise his eyes to heaven; but he beat his breast and said, 'God be merciful to me, a sinner.'

Luke 18.11–13, Jerusalem Bible

Here is a true story. A Catholic woman was one of a handful of people who went to her church for Mass seven days a week. She was respected and admired for this. One night she called the priest and urgently begged him to come to the hospital where her daughter, Louise, lay badly beaten up. When he arrived he was surprised to find Ann, whom he had always thought of as a modest, devout woman, yelling and swearing and threatening vengeance. She shouted like a harridan: 'I'll kill him! I'll murder him!' She hadn't noticed the priest come in but she suddenly turned on her daughter who lay still on the bed. 'Anyway, it's your fault, Louise,' she cried. 'It serves you right, you slut! You *will* do that disgusting work! Huh! A daughter of mine a prostitute!'

Then she noticed the priest and her demeanour changed completely. 'Oh, good evening, Father,' she said. 'It's good of you to come.'

He just smiled and went over to the girl. He was horrified at what he saw. 'How are you feeling?' he asked. Her face was so badly smashed that she had difficulty in speaking, but she managed a shaky smile. 'It wasn't really his fault,' she said.

After he told the story of the Pharisee and the tax collector, Jesus said of the tax collector, 'I tell you, this man went home at rights with God; the other did not.'

Was it Ann or Louise who was more at rights with God?

* * *

Joy 1

You show me the path of life.
In your presence there is fulness of joy;
in your right hand are pleasures forevermore.
Psalm 16.11

I have been told that one Sunday, at the beginning of Mass in St Patrick's Cathedral in New York, each member of the congregation was given a helium-filled balloon. They were asked to release their balloon when they felt joy. At the end of Mass most people were still holding their balloons. What does this tell us about that congregation, or about us, because I guess that the same thing would happen in most Anglican and Catholic churches throughout the west?

Things are different in some of the Free churches. I think particularly of the Pentecostals, who express so much joy and enthusiasm in their worship. And what of the Catholic and

Anglican churches in developing countries? Mass in Africa is scarcely recognizable as the same celebration as we have in Europe. 'Celebration' describes the worship there more accurately than it does our Sunday ritual. Their faces are alight; they dance and sing for joy, whereas we sit dutifully and rather numbly in our places.

Someone might ask: 'What is there to be joyful about? The world is in a terrible state: climate change, the nuclear threat, thousands of children dying of hunger, dysentery, AIDS and violence everywhere.' And at a more personal level a woman might say, 'How can I be joyful? My sister is dying, my son is in prison, my husband has been made redundant.'

Yet no-one can doubt that the people in Africa and other countries who worship God with true joy are faced with the same problems as we are. What are horrific statistics to us are reality for them. It is their own children who are dying of hunger, their own parents who are dying of AIDS. The difference is that for them the gospel of Jesus is fresh and alive.

* * *

Joy 2

One of my own experiences of a Christian service filled with joy was actually in England. A few of us had spent a long weekend listening to a group of young people and talking with them about God and about themselves. We let go our defences and got to know one another at depth.

At the end of the weekend we held a paraliturgy in the choir of Gloucester Cathedral mainly put together by the young people. It was a winter evening, and the blaze of candle flame in the centre of our circle was the only light in that awesome place. Everyone was absorbed in the worship; the youngest among us forbore to giggle and the oldest to behave too sedately. At the 'sign of peace' which resembled an outsize rugby scrum, we nonetheless miraculously avoided tripping over the candles, and by contrast the long period of silence was profound. There was an almost tangible atmosphere of joy. At the end we walked out in single file along the cloister, each carrying a lighted candle and singing 'Walk, walk, in the Light.'

The ancient cloister at Gloucester is one of the most beautiful anywhere, and it must have been a rare event in that hallowed place when, rather than a solemn procession of dignified prelates, a line of relatively scruffy youngsters made their way along, their faces lit with gladness.

Of course, we can feel joy without singing and dancing and shouting. Perhaps all we need do is silently focus on Jesus Christ and the amazing gift that he is when he comes to meet us in the Eucharist.

* * *

Positive attitude

The LORD God appointed a bush, and made it come up over Jonah, to give shade over his head, to save him from his discomfort; so Jonah was very happy about the bush. But when dawn came up the next day, God appointed a worm that attacked the bush, so that it withered.

Jonah 4.6–7

The story of Jonah is humorous. It tells the story of this unlikely prophet Jonah and his comic adventures. He defies God, gets stuck in the belly of a whale, and when his mission is successfully completed he grumbles and sulks, is critical of God and cross with him. In return, God teases him with the bush and the worm.

Our friend Walter isn't at all like Jonah. There isn't a grumpy bone in his body. We first met him in London, when he was working in an inner-city area. We invited him to come and stay in our cottage in the country.

As the time of his visit drew nearer, we planned to make it as pleasant a few days as possible. Although it was rather late in October, I was glad to see that most of the trees were still resplendent in their colours, and the garden was looking beautiful. However, Walter arrived in the thickest fog we had seen for years. You couldn't even make out the house from the gate. I greeted him warmly but rather nervously. 'I'm so sorry about this awful weather,' I apologized. Walter smiled broadly. 'But I love it!' he exclaimed, 'I just love the weather, all weather!' As the weekend developed we came to understand Walter; his words 'I just love the weather' kept recurring to me, and I realized he meant it.

Walter doesn't just accept things, he delights in them. He delights in fog, and in sunshine, in eating a delicious meal and in washing up afterwards. He approaches everything with expectant joy. And this is infectious: you can't be with Walter for long without feeling happy.

The fourteenth-century Meister Eckhart wrote, 'Wisdom consists of doing the next thing you have to do, doing it with your whole heart and finding delight in doing it.'

Now, when I'm caught in a downpour or have to clean the oven, I remember Walter gratefully, for he is one of the people who is leading me nearer to God.

* * *

Little children

> Then little children were being brought to him in order that he might lay his hands on them and pray. The disciples spoke sternly to those who brought them, but Jesus said, 'Let the little children come to me, and do not stop them, for it is to such as these that the kingdom of heaven belongs.'
>
> Matthew 19.13–14

I wished I had my camera with me when I saw Lily and Emma. They would have made a touching picture, and more importantly for me, they provided some sort of answer to a question that had been puzzling me for a long time.

St Matthew tells us that when the disciples sternly turned the children away, no doubt thinking he was overtired, Jesus told them to allow them to come to him, because 'it is to such as these that the kingdom of heaven belongs'.

I have often pondered on this story. As a mother and teacher for many, many years I have known a lot of children, and it's impossible to deny that by and large, for all their endearing qualities, they can nonetheless be self-centred, greedy and sometimes even spiteful.

Lily and Emma are five years old. Lily is totally blind, and Emma, a diminutive Down's syndrome child with owlish spectacles and long silky hair, had taken her hand and was leading her gently and gravely round the corner to the classroom.

Emma wasn't trying to impress anybody, nor was she playing a game. She was just loving another person, and truly of such is the kingdom of heaven.

* * *

Personal peace 1

Peace I leave with you; my peace I give to you. I do not give to you as the world gives. Do not let your hearts be troubled, and do not let them be afraid.

John 14.27

How does a woman feel when she hears that her child is dead, or when she discovers a lump in her breast? How does a man feel when he is suddenly made redundant, or finds that his loved and trusted wife wants to leave him for someone else? First, there is the swift pain of shock, and then fear takes its grip. Involved with the fear are other, different emotions, varying with the person and the circumstances: anger, dismay, disbelief and so on. But underneath, struggling to emerge, there is the determination to survive, to hold on to sanity, and to regain a state of peace.

When the angel came and told Mary that she was to be the mother of God's son, she was shocked and frightened. She wasn't just startled by the vision, but afraid of what was being asked of her. In a few seconds her world had been turned upside down, her dreams of a happy uncomplicated marriage shattered, and a terrifying responsibility laid on her.

Mary was good; she had absolute faith in God and so she probably didn't hesitate before she submitted to his will. 'Here am I, the servant of the Lord; let it be with me according to your word.'

Her submission was perfect and immediate, but we can never know how long it took and how much it cost before her acceptance was complete.

* * *

Personal peace 2

Young people, those who are wise enough not to set their sights on wealth, power or popularity, naturally long for happiness and love. As we grow older, we change; of all things, peace seems the most desirable. It's not that we're settling for less; we know that peace will not be ours without love, and that true joy only comes where there is peace. It's the 'pearl without price', almost impossible to find yet worth all the striving. It was the gift that Jesus left behind for us: 'My peace I give to you.'

I imagine that after the Annunciation, the peace which Mary would have experienced was a certain stillness within, but not a negative state. This kind of peace is joyful and alive. Nor is it static; it must reach out to affect those around.

In the first place, this peace must, as the song says, begin with me. Like Mary waiting on God and feeling close to him, I must offer him my life as it is now, my hopes, my fears, my dreams, my hurts and my longings. And if I have just had a shock, if I am afraid of death, betrayal, another's suffering or an uncertain future, I must offer these too. In this way, slowly and painfully, I may begin to accept, and acceptance is the beginning of peace within. As with Mary at the Annunciation, true peace does not mean running away or being insulated from the problems of life, but facing up to life joyfully and with courage, trusting that God's strength will support us. And there can be no peace without justice. As long as there is violence, oppression, hunger, poverty, war or injustice of any kind anywhere in the world, no follower of Christ can be truly at peace.

* * *

A watered garden

They shall come and sing aloud on the height of Zion,
and they shall be radiant over the goodness of the LORD,
over the grain, the wine and the oil,
and over the young of the flock and the herd;
their life shall become like a watered garden,
and they shall never languish again.

Jeremiah 31.12

I watch the television news. I see and hear what is happening in the world and I am appalled, angered, sickened and disgusted. I want to switch off, but I have to know.

Another country invaded in the name of somebody's rights; another aggressive act perpetrated against humanity; more people maimed, killed, bereaved; maniacs, pitiless and terrifying, raping someone's daughter or murdering someone's son; imprisonment and torture of the innocent and the brave; a family of children burnt to death in their home.

Among my friends Jill, Mervyn, Edna and Anne, Jill has had a breakdown and yesterday she was taken into hospital. Mervyn, whose two wives have both left him, has discovered that his only son is on heroin. Edna is dying of cancer and Anne has just been jilted by the man she loves.

This morning I walked out into the sunshine and my heart was filled with joy. How can this be? Am I indifferent to what is happening in the world? Do I care so little about Jill and Mervyn and Edna and Anne? Don't I have to be insensitive to be happy in such a world? Am I so absorbed in myself that what happens to my friends impinges so little on me?

It seems to me that my life is like a watered garden, filled with an abundance of God's gifts and the power of growth. I know sorrow, yes, I feel it for my friends; and I also know beauty and delight, friendship and affection, wonder and the desire to be alive and creative.

I'm not joyful because I don't care; I'm joyful because my God gives me so much that my cup overflows, because he has made my life so rich, rich in sorrow and love and joy.

* * *

Blasphemy

. . . the angel said to them, 'Do not be afraid, for see – I am bringing you good news of great joy for all the people: to you is born this day in the city of David a Saviour, who is the Messiah, the Lord. This will be a sign for you: you will find a child wrapped in bands of cloth and lying in a manger.'
Luke 2.10–12

I suppose I have seen representations of this scene at least a thousand times, in paintings and sculpture, on Christmas cards and in nativity plays.

But today our good friends Becca and Ian gave us something different: a nativity scene on a Christmas card that surprised and momentarily even shocked me. It was a photograph of Becca, dressed in pale blue, with their new baby Matilda on her lap, Ian, wearing a Middle-Eastern head-dress, standing at her side, and Ben, their black labrador, imperfectly disguised as a lamb, a sheepskin sliding off his back, standing in front of the group.

Startled, I thought, 'Surely this is a kind of blasphemy.' But then I realized that no, this too was God incarnate, the love that came down at Christmas. For surely in their love for one another and for Matilda, in the generosity and kindness and warmth of this young couple, there is a place fit for the indwelling of Christ. As we sometimes sing, 'Where is love and loving-kindness, God is fain to dwell.'

Becca and Ian are 'loving and giving' more than most people I know, yet they are not churchgoers, in no way religious. We are asked to evangelize, to spread the good news about Christianity, but how can I do this? I would love Becca and Ian to know God, but how am I to teach them? I could try, as I do, to live a Christ-like life, but isn't it presumptuous and patronizing to expect them to learn from this when the lives these young people lead may well be more Christ-like than mine?

I conclude that what matters is that God loves them and me equally, and that they, in their being and doing, are in tune with his Spirit. As for me, I guess I have to try and fail and try again to be the person God wants me to be.

* * *

Bright eyes 1

The eyes of the Lord are on those who love him,
a mighty shield and strong support,
a shelter from scorching wind and a shade from
*   noonday sun,*
a guard against stumbling and a help against falling.
He lifts up the soul and makes the eyes sparkle;
he gives health and life and blessing.

Sirach 34.19–20

These lines from Sirach are a wonderful description of some of God's attributes, but I couldn't help a wry smile because just after I read them I happened to stumble over a high kerb and fell to the ground with a thud. I don't believe that the God I love will prevent me from having accidents, but I do believe in his love for me. Yet what I specially like about this passage is the assurance that God makes our eyes sparkle.

It doesn't matter what a person's face is like: scarred and disfigured, old and blotched and wrinkled or flawless in its beauty, what moves us most is the light in the eyes.

Our eyes brighten when we receive a lovely surprise, when we see something exceptionally beautiful, when we recognize a friend we haven't seen for a long time, or when we are concentrating on something that holds our interest. People in love sometimes seem to have a permanent sparkle in their eyes.

And when we sit quietly with God, listening to him, open to his inspiration, our eyes will be as bright as though we are gazing into his face.

* * *

Bright eyes 2

I went to see Flora in the nursing home.
I didn't really want to go to visit her,
but someone told me she was very frail now
and I knew if I didn't go
I'd be overwhelmed with guilt when she died.

Flora had always been good to me.
She was generous and funny and very astute.
Her face was lovely and her eyes
blue as the sea on a summer's day.

It was some years since I'd seen her.
I knew she'd have changed.
I prepared myself for a shock,
but when I saw her I wanted to cry.

She sat in a chair, wrapped in shawls,
head bent, pink scalp visible under the wisps of
    white hair,
hands mottled and gnarled.
I bent down and took her cold hand in mine.
I said, 'Flora?'
She raised her head then
and looked at me steadily.
She was no longer attractive,

she who had been so beautiful.
The blue of her eyes had faded.
But the moment she recognized me
those eyes brightened,
her old sparkle was there
and she smiled.

* * *

Evangelization

Go therefore, and make disciples of all nations.
Matthew 28.19

A few years ago, the Christian churches announced that there
was to be a Decade of Evangelism. Those ten years have come
and gone, and sadly there is little evidence of the fruits of this
enterprise, at any rate in sophisticated western countries. I
suspect that until Christians are united themselves, they are
unlikely to attract many others to their faith.

St Francis is reputed to have said: 'Preach the gospel at all
times, and as a last resort, use words.' Over the years I have heard
ministers and priests preaching a similar message from different pulpits: 'You don't have to go round telling people about
Jesus, you just have to be a shining example of Christianity.'

I thought about that. It isn't as easy as it sounds. How can
I be a shining example of anything, when so many agnostics
and atheists I know are more generous and more committed
to good works than I am?

I soon realized that it would be counter-productive to attempt
to proselytize in any way. The people in our country who have
problems such as crippling debt, homelessness or severe depres-
sion are no more able to take in the Good News than the desperately hungry in Africa. Other issues have to be addressed first, and
would-be 'missionaries' have to become politically involved.
We have to take action, writing letters to our Member of
Parliament and joining with others to protest against injustice.

I have tried to do all these things, which I hope will help the people I befriend, but I cannot deceive myself into believing it is any sort of evangelization.

The people who really evangelize go a lot further than I do. They live among those who know nothing of Jesus Christ. They become one with the people, just as Jesus himself became one with us. It is these ordinary people of extraordinary selflessness – I think of the Salvation Army and the Little Sisters and Brothers of Jesus – that truly contribute to the spreading of the Good News.

* * *

Worry

But the Lord answered: 'Martha, Martha,' he said, 'you worry and fret about so many things.'

Luke 10.41, Jerusalem Bible

Martha's husband, David, usually took a long evening walk after a stressful day in his city office. Normally he was back by eight o'clock, just in time for supper. But one Wednesday when there was still no sign of him at half past eight, Martha began to worry in earnest. By nine o'clock she had rung round all his friends in their village, his local and their hospital. She was feeling angry. By a quarter past, her annoyance had changed to grief. What if David had been killed in a traffic accident or been the victim of a serious mugging? He might have been kidnapped . . .

She realized her imagination was in overdrive and to calm herself began to plan the funeral. She had just decided on the last hymn and was about to choose a venue for the reception afterwards when she heard David's key turning in the lock.

Martha rushed out to meet him and to his surprise flung her arms round him and burst into tears. He dried her tears and patiently explained that he had bumped into Geoff, an old friend who was looking miserable, having recently been divorced. Feeling sorry for Geoff, he had agreed to go to his club for a chat.

'It took much longer than I thought it would,' he said, 'and I'm absolutely ravenous. Let's have supper.'

Martha's face fell. 'Oh dear,' she said, 'I'm sorry, David, but I was so worried, I forgot to switch the oven on. It will be another hour, I'm afraid.'

David laughed. 'Martha, Martha,' he said, 'you worry and fret about so many things!'

And Martha blushed, thinking, 'We haven't changed much since Jesus walked on the earth.'

* * *

Keeping up appearances

We are not commending ourselves to you again, but giving you an opportunity to boast about us, so that you may be able to answer those who boast in outward appearance and not in the heart.

2 Corinthians 5.12

When my top front tooth (a crown) fell out, I panicked. I looked in the mirror and thought I looked hideous. Hastily I phoned my dentist and he kindly agreed to see me that same morning and fitted me with a temporary repair.

When I heard that the new Archbishop of York was from Uganda I was delighted, partly because it would do away with the rather stuffy image some people have of the Church of England, but mainly because I have a particular fondness for African and Afro-Caribbean people, possibly owing to the fact that our adopted son is black. I made sure I watched the television news that evening, but when I saw John Sentamu's face with the big gap in his front teeth, I have to confess that I was shocked, and I felt sorry for him. Poor man! I thought, he must not have had time to get that big gap fixed.

Next time he appeared on television, however, I realized that he isn't vain like me. In any case his big friendly smile more than compensates for his less-than-perfect teeth. Perhaps he doesn't think appearance is that important, or perhaps he identifies with the poor who can't afford a dentist, or both. In any case, he made me feel rather silly and shallow, and he made me admire him the more.

So I was very cross when I overheard a prominent member of our congregation, who had been invited to his Installation, remark that it was 'an extraordinary shambles and totally out of keeping for an ancient, beautiful building like York Minster'. I had seen the Installation too, but only on television. I thought it was wonderful, inspired and inspiring, explosive with life. And I feel pretty sure God thought so too.

* * *

Respectability

The Son of Man came eating and drinking, and they say, 'Look, a glutton and a drunkard, a friend of tax collectors and sinners!'

Matthew 11.19

I think I am generally considered to be a respectable person. I try not to go out unless my hair is combed and my shoes polished. And when I go to church on Sundays, I am extra respectable. I discard my rather scruffy everyday jacket for my best overcoat and sometimes even wear a hat. I don't use obscene or blasphemous language (at any rate not in anyone's hearing!) and I don't forget to say 'please' and 'thank you'.

I was brought up to believe that such things are important, but now I can see that my respectable behaviour is not part of my witness or my fulfilment as a Christian. On the contrary, preoccupation with such niceties is actually sinful, since it might prevent me from paying full attention to the needs and wishes and dreams of others.

I believe that Jesus spent time with tax collectors, prostitutes and sinners, not in the hope of persuading them to be respectable, nor with the intention of setting them a good example. He spent time with them because he loved them and wanted them to understand that God loved them unconditionally. I guess he also enjoyed their company.

We 'good' churchgoers receive the astonishing gift of Jesus himself in the Eucharist. Then what do we do? Probably we thank him with full hearts before going home to resume our respectable lives, keeping him locked in our hearts, not allowing his love to overflow from us and touch our neighbour – our neighbour who doesn't believe in God, perhaps, or who is cynical about Christianity, the one who is overwhelmed by problems he cannot solve, or the one who is enduring grief, the magnitude of which we can only guess at. And then there is the neighbour we find insignificant and dull. Are we willing to let Christ's Spirit loose on her?

It's so easy to be nice and respectable, so easy to confuse this with being true followers of Christ. He has given us himself – that is, everything. What he asks in return is not the nothingness of respectability.

* * *

Spring 1

> *Arise, my love, my fair one*
> *and come away;*
> *for now the winter is past,*
> *the rain is over and gone.*
> *The flowers appear on the earth:*
> *the time of singing has come,*
> *and the voice of the turtledove*
> *is heard in our land.*
> The Song of Solomon 2.10–12

I love summer when there is such an abundance of flowers with all their different shapes and colours and scents. I love autumn when the trees are so poignantly lovely, and winter when they stand noble in their nakedness and sometimes the snow falls softly and gently muffles everything.

But I agree with the poet Gerard Manley Hopkins when he says, 'Nothing is so beautiful as spring.' It begins, just tentatively, in January, when so often the sky is grey and the trees and the earth itself are black. Looking for the first white tips of snowdrops and the yellow buds of winter aconites, watching in early February for the birds to begin their frantic nest-building and listening for their cheery excited conversations, I feel the first pang of sadness, fearing that all this loveliness of spring will rush by too fast and merge into summer.

For me the season, with its revelation of one delight after another, unfolds too quickly. No sooner are the snowdrops fully out than the wild daffodils appear, to be followed almost at once by primroses and bluebells; and before we know it, fresh leaves are appearing on the trees.

* * *

Spring 2

I cannot slow the passage of the seasons, but I can slow down the pace of my life. So now every year I try to make small pilgrimages which take no more than half a day. A real pilgrimage, of course, is a journey, often arduous, which focuses on the end, the climax, maybe the shrine of a saint, and in some way brings us closer to God, increasing our devotion and often our sense of being cleansed and forgiven. My own spring pilgrimages are much simpler and less ambitious, but they also bring me closer to God because the loveliness of the flowers lifts my mind and heart to worship and adore their creator. On the first day I have set aside, I walk slowly, glorying in God's creation, to the tiny, hidden hamlet where someone has planted a zillion snowdrops along the lane and on every patch of grass.

Soon it's the time to wander alongside the little River Dove where wild daffodils cram the banks on either side. A little later I walk in the high lonely wood where primroses grow in profusion, and last I climb to the grassy bank far from any road where I gaze on the misty blue of a sea of bluebells.

The beauty of each of these places is almost unbearable for me, and I thank God over and over again because I am blessed with the health and strength and knowledge to walk to these places and share them with my friends. When I stand looking at these flowers I am filled with wonder, love and praise.

* * *

Compassion

The Lord is compassion and love,
slow to anger and rich in mercy.
Psalm 103.8, Grail Psalms

The God who loves and whom we love is the all-compassionate one. Compassion is much more than pity; it is the aspect of love which means 'suffering with'. In our turn, we who bear the name of Christ respond to this love by trying to be compassionate ourselves: we seek out the lonely and visit the sick, we campaign for justice, because we are moved by pity for the weak and oppressed, the hungry, the victims of torture, imprisonment and violence.

But it is a mistake to think we have a monopoly on this. The followers of the world's great religions show it too. For instance, compassion is central to the teachings of both Buddhism and Islam.

It may be legitimate for us to think of ourselves as compassionate when we care enough about others to take action on their behalf. But there is a risk that we may fall into the trap of imagining that we are 'the good people' condescending to feel compassion even on sinners.

We could hardly continue to hold such an attitude after reading what Dennis Skillicorn has written. He is a prisoner on Death Row in America – in other words, someone condemned to die because of the gravity of his crime. He is writing about a magazine started with some of his fellow lifers:

Even from the inside of a maximum-security prison, there are ways to make a positive difference. For example,

44

Compassion is a bi-monthly publication created, written and edited by death row offenders to raise scholarship money for family members of murdered victims. It also gives those living life on death row a chance to share their artistic and social expression and to contribute to their culture in a positive way. They share life lessons in the hope that others who read their material will not make the same bad choices they made. They write about the importance of forgiveness, reconciliation, restitution and restorative justice. They share their regrets, their remorse . . . and their dreams.

Surely this is a living testimony to the way the Holy Spirit works in the human spirit.

* * *

Light

In him was life, and the life was the light of all people. The light shines in the darkness, and the darkness did not overcome it.

John 1.4–5

Of the four Gospel writers, John is at times the least easy to understand, perhaps because he is the only one we might call 'mystical'.

When I read that Jesus said to his disciples: 'You are the light of the world' (Matthew 5.14), I feel the same sense of unworthiness and disbelief. I find it very hard to grasp that Jesus, our Light, is within me. Sometimes I have glimpsed in the eyes of others the light of joy, the light of hope, the light of truth, of compassion. Far more than the flickering candle which dispels the darkness around me, this is the true light of Christ.

It is part of the great mystery of our God, that he who dwells 'beyond the very highest heavens', beyond the furthest stars in the universe, yet lives as the light in the dancing eyes of a child.

I walked in the rain, not looking up at the sky
or around at the trees but down at the ground,
the grey muddy ground.
I saw a puddle, and stopped,
for there was a rainbow, there was every colour,
there was light.
And I thought of Jesus
who shines everywhere, anywhere,
even in puddles,
even, can it be so? in me?

* * *

Gift

*Now there are a variety of gifts, but the same Spirit; and
there are varieties of services, but the same Lord; and there
are varieties of activities, but it is the same God who acti-
vates all of them in everyone.*

1 Corinthians 12.4–6

'Mam! He's doing it again!' Ged remembers his young daughter
saying this to her mother because he, without realizing what
he was doing, was sculpting the mashed potatoes on his plate
into marvellous shapes. His children laughed at him then, but
they loved it when he helped them to build their snowman,
because theirs was by far the most captivating one in the
neighbourhood, having so many beautiful accessories shaped
out of the snow by their father.

Ged himself gave little thought to this. He didn't think of
himself as having any particular talent, and at school he had
been labelled useless at Art. Then one day he brought home a piece
of driftwood that he liked the look of, and idly, hardly conscious
of what he was doing, he picked up a Stanley knife and began
changing the shape of the wood. He was 43 years old, and this
was the beginning of Ged's creative wood-carving.

Very soon friends, then art shop owners, then galleries, were asking for his work. One day someone asked him to make a box for an old lady as a container for rosary beads. Ged made a square box, then cut out a circle to hold the lid. He thought, 'This isn't good enough,' so he carved a cross inside the box. Still it didn't satisfy him, and he decided to carve a face and figure of Jesus. The wood was very hard and resistant to his knife. Ged struggled for a while, then, he told us, he spoke aloud to God, saying, 'You're not making this easy for me, are you?' At once, the wood became curiously soft, 'Just like Edam cheese,' Ged said, and he completed the carving easily and quickly. But when he touched the finished figure, the wood was hard again.

Ged wasn't sure whether he believed in miracles or not, but he was sure of the look on the old lady's face when she saw the box.

* * *

Harvest

Very truly, I tell you, unless a grain of wheat falls into the earth and dies, it remains just a single grain; but if it dies, it bears much fruit.

John 12.24

As I understand it, in this passage Jesus is saying, somewhat para-doxically, that if we want to lead full and fruitful lives we have to die to self. This means subduing our obsession with our own comfort, welfare and reputation and taking risks for the sake of others.

With my husband, Chris, I belong to a small group of people who meet regularly in Lent to discuss different topics. We were asked to lead a session on justice, and we decided to challenge our friends by presenting them with certain imaginary situations and asking them how they would respond.

The first scenario went something like this: 'You are walking home one very cold night when you bump into a stranger who is looking lost. You ask him if he is all right and he tells you he has nowhere to sleep. What do you do?'

The more articulate members of the group responded first. They all said roughly the same thing, the sort of thing I would have said myself: 'I would have felt really sorry for him but I wouldn't have been able to bring myself to offer him a bed. He might have been on drugs, or be a dangerous criminal on the run. He might steal or break things. I know it's not being like Jesus, which is what we are meant to be, but . . . !'

It seemed we were all more or less in agreement, when Joan, one of a quiet couple who don't usually have much to contribute, said musingly: 'We've never had any trouble, have we, Gerry?' It turned out that Gerry and Joan regularly welcome tramps and down-and-outs into their home, if necessary giving them a bed, and think it's a perfectly normal thing to do.

Afterwards, I thought of all the people who over the years must have been warmed and blessed by the selfless kindness of this unassuming couple. Their lives have indeed borne much fruit.

* * *

Odd man out 1

All who saw it began to grumble and said, 'He has gone to be the guest of one who is a sinner.'

Luke 19.7

The people complained because Jesus had decided to go to the house of Zaccheus, whom they despised. They didn't like him because he was a tax collector, and (as still happens here!) all tax collectors were considered to be bad men. Certainly a great many of them grew rich through cheating the people, and Zaccheus was probably one of those, because he so willingly confessed his guilt and was ready to make amends.

48

He seems to have been something of an outsider. He wanted to see Jesus when he came through Jericho, but because he was a small man he couldn't see over the heads of the crowds. Presumably his unpopularity meant that nobody would let him through to the front, so he climbed a tree instead. At least he showed enterprise and had determination, but we can guess that some people laughed at the little man up in the tree.

In our society it is not tax collectors who are the target of concentrated hate and revulsion, but paedophiles. It's easy to see why: it's because our children are so precious and parents have an understandable dread of the stranger (though in fact it is very often *not* a stranger) who might abuse and attack their sons or daughters. Sadly, sometimes fear and dislike develop into hysteria, as in the case of people who confused 'paedophile' with 'paediatrician' and mobbed a completely innocent doctor. Not surprisingly, many people find it almost impossible to try to understand the terrible compulsion that drives people to perpetrate such horrific acts.

* * *

Odd man out 2

One autumn day I had an unusual encounter. I had been for a long walk in the park and was tired – I needed to sit down. It was a lovely day and the benches were fully occupied, except one where a man was sitting by himself. I didn't really want to sit by him; there seemed to be something rather sinister about him. His face was very white and he was wearing a big, shabby black coat. He was staring straight ahead of him, without expression. I told myself not to be silly – after all, there were plenty of people about. So I sat down beside him.

After a while I made some comment about the weather. We exchanged a few words, and then I asked him if he lived in the town. Suddenly he began to talk, speaking in a low voice, matter-of-fact and without self-pity.

'No, I don't live in the town; I don't live anywhere. I have to keep moving on, because there's nowhere safe. I'm a paedophile, you see,' and he waited for my reaction. When I said nothing, he went on, 'People don't understand, Miss, and I don't expect you do, but I can't help it, I just can't. It's a kind of compulsion and they say there's no cure. You don't know how I hate myself, much more than other folk hate me. I've got no family, no friends, but I don't blame anybody else. I do pray. I pray to Jesus. Do you believe in Jesus?'

'Yes,' I said, 'yes I do. And I will pray for you.'

'Thank you,' he said, then he stood up. 'I must move on. Thank you for listening.'

I realized then that he wasn't sinister at all. He had a quiet dignity about him. Very hesitantly he held out his hand towards me, and when I took it he seemed moved. On an impulse I reached up and kissed him on the cheek. He blushed then, and smiled faintly, and as I walked away I wondered how many years it had been since he'd been embraced.

* * *

Mother

Jerusalem, Jerusalem, the city that kills the prophets and stones those who are sent to it! How often have I desired to gather your children together as a hen gathers her brood under her wings, and you were not willing!

Luke 13.34

This image which Jesus uses of the mother hen is remarkable. It is true that his stories were always built around things which were homely and familiar to the people of his day, and what could be more homely and familiar then or now than chickens and hens?

What surprises us is that he applies the image of the mother hen to himself. Jesus was not a fussy old woman; we are accustomed to thinking of him as a strong young man, so his simile is particularly striking. What is more, in this rather beautiful illustration, he casts himself in the role of a mother.

The phrase 'Jesus, our mother' is at first sight somewhat disconcerting. But it is one with which Julian of Norwich, the fourteenth-century English mystic, was comfortable. In recording the visions that were revealed to her, she wrote:

> A mother's caring is the closest, nearest and surest for it is the truest. This care never might, nor could, nor should be done fully except by him alone . . . our true mother, Jesus, who is all love, bears us into joy and endless living . . . a mother feeds her child with her milk, but our beloved mother Jesus feeds us with himself.

What moves me, and perhaps most mothers, about this heartfelt cry of Jesus is the way I can identify with a mother's acute longing to protect and help her wayward children. The people of Jerusalem did not heed the words of Jesus, and so often our children are not willing to listen to our advice. All mothers and fathers have to learn the hard lesson of letting go, but the fierce longing to gather our offspring under our wings again seldom goes away.

* * *

Weakness

[The Lord] said to me, 'My grace is sufficient for you, for power is made perfect in weakness.' So, I will boast all the more gladly of my weaknesses, so that the power of Christ may dwell in me.

2 Corinthians 12.9

The other day I came across a very weak creature. I was high up on the moors and when I turned the corner of a drystone wall, there was a ewe with two lambs just newly born and tiny. One was already upright and ready to feed, but as I watched, the smaller one struggled over and over to stand, almost getting there only to tumble over again.

At last he managed to stand, his black woolly legs splayed but steady now, and thankfully I went on my way. A lamb is, of course, one of the symbols of Jesus Christ, and so it should be, for the one who is our Lord and our God is also the vulnerable one, the one we ignore, take for granted, fail to listen to, fail to respond to. We neglect him, we forget him, day after day we wound him with our lack of love.

Yet he is Jesus, the one who wants to be our brother and our friend, the one who gave us his body and his blood, who was crucified for our redemption.

Since Jesus Christ knows what it is to be vulnerable and weak, he is able to identify with us in our weakness; he knows what it is like to suffer. When we are ill, bereaved, depressed, rejected or in pain, when, like the lamb I stumbled upon today, we struggle for life itself, he is there with us. And when, as Christians, we are feeble and pathetic, forsaking him again and again, perhaps even in us, in *our* weakness, his power may sometimes be shown.

* * *

Reconciliation 1

When Esau heard his father's words, he cried out with an exceedingly great and bitter cry, and said to his father, 'Bless me, me also, father!' But he said, 'Your brother came deceitfully and he has taken away your blessing.'

Genesis 27.34–35

Deliver me, please, from the hand of my brother, from the hand of Esau, for I am afraid of him; he may come and kill us all.

Genesis 32.11

But Esau ran to meet him, and embraced him, and fell on his neck and kissed him, and they wept.

Genesis 33.4

The story of Esau and Jacob is full of drama, and much too long to use here, but it gives us a wonderful example of reconciliation. Jacob stole his twin brother's birthright, a terrible sin compounded by cruelty and deceit. Understandably, Esau was furiously angry and vowed vengeance. Jacob fled to his uncle's home, where he stayed for 20 years. Eventually he decided to return, although he was very much afraid to meet his brother and expected to be killed.

But Esau did not stand on ceremony or even treat Jacob coldly. Instead, like the father in the story of the prodigal son, he ran to meet him and threw his arms around him.

Most of us find reconciliation difficult. We are held back by stubbornness and pride. A close friend of mine quarrelled with her only son and they didn't speak for years, until both had forgotten the reason why. Then my friend had a heart attack and died. The son rushed to her bedside but he was too late. He was devastated by guilt and grief. 'If only I had picked up the phone!' he said. 'If only . . .'

* * *

Reconciliation 2

There is a story, also true, which has a different ending, and which I have told many times because I find it very moving.

Ray had flown a bomber during the Second World War. He was instructed to 'knock the hell out of' a small town, Kleve, in north Germany. Conditions were just right, and they scored direct hits and destroyed much of the centre of the town as well as a big church. With his crew Ray watched the buildings collapse and burst into flames. They grinned at one another. 'Success!' they gloated.

But over the years, as he matured, Ray began to see this incident very differently. He began to have nightmares about

53

the people he had killed in that German town. It took him years, but eventually he managed to summon up the courage to write a letter to the Burgermeister of the town, explaining who he was and asking to be forgiven. The letter was given to the parish priest, and in the church (by now rebuilt) the following Sunday, he read Ray's letter to the congregation and then invited those who were willing to forgive Ray to sign their names on a return letter. Everyone signed. Some weeks later Ray went out to meet the survivors of his raid and the relatives of the victims. This was a struggle for Ray and for several of those affected, but in the end they all forgave him and so were reconciled. Ray had great physical courage as a young man, even greater moral courage in his later years.

The effect of Ray's action was far-reaching. He was not the only one to be reconciled.

Gradually, an exchange system was built up, not only between the people of Ray's home town and the German town he had bombed, but between the Anglicans of his own parish and the Catholics of the restored church. So as a result of one man's initiative, friendships blossomed and reconciliation grew between Germans and British, and Christians of different churches. It was a remarkable instance of the 'ripple effect', the power of one apparently small initiative to spread forgiveness and peace among communities.

* * *

Surprise

> *The wilderness and the dry land shall be glad,*
> *the desert shall rejoice and blossom;*
> *like the crocus it shall blossom abundantly*
> *and rejoice with joy and singing.*
>
> Isaiah 35.1–2

One of the countless ways in which God blesses us is by giving us surprises and unexpected joys.

Today I was surprised and delighted by something totally unexpected when I was on a long walk in a quiet Yorkshire dale. This walk, on this day, didn't have a lot going for it. It had rained on us all morning and the ground was soggy underfoot; both my boots let in the muddy water. We had forgotten our gloves and our hands were blue and numb with cold. Worst of all was the wind. It was bitter and fierce, so that at one point I was quite frightened by its strength and felt I could be lifted off my feet.

We had a small picnic with us, just a sandwich and a chocolate bar. But there was nowhere we could sit down to eat it, or even find shelter from the wind. In the end we huddled in a corner between two grey stone buildings, and tried to keep the rain off our food.

Afterwards we continued on our walk down a muddy lane, dodging puddles and cowpats and walking as fast as we could with the idea of getting the walk over as soon as possible and reaching somewhere warm.

Then Chris saw the garden. We had come across no signs of spring, other than a few clumps of bedraggled snowdrops, all day, but here was something different. Suddenly, there was such brightness and colour, not from a mass of blossom but from tiny delicate flowers: pale mauve crocuses, a miniature iris, a trout lily and other rare and lovely blooms for which I have no name.

It was a delightful surprise, a gift, and the best encouragement for perseverance on our way. We stopped hankering for the end of our walk and instead relished the joyous present moment.

* * *

Sunshine

But I say to you, Love your enemies and pray for those who persecute you, so that you may be children of your Father in heaven, for he makes his sun rise on the evil and on the good . . .

Matthew 5.44–45

The sun shines on everyone, and everyone except the blind and perhaps those locked away in prison can enjoy the benefit of its light. Spiritually speaking, Jesus is the Light of the world, and physically speaking, the natural phenomenon that is the sun is the light of the world. It brings not only light but life and warmth and healing, yet we take it for granted.

When I lived in India, for the first few weeks of my arrival I would exclaim, as soon as I got up in the morning, 'What a beautiful day!' It took me a while to realize that every day, except during the brief monsoon, was made beautiful by constant sunshine. But here in England, the sun shone yesterday for the first time in weeks after a long spell of cold, grey weather, and it seemed as though everyone in town was smiling.

Our God bestows the warmth of his love on all his children; he gives us light and life and healing, and he looks with compassion on saints and sinners alike.

This sad but beautiful poem was found on the base of a cross erected in Normandy in 1632:

> I am the great sun, but you do not see me,
> I am the husband, but you turn away.
> I am the captive, but you do not free me,
> I am the captain, but you will not obey,
> I am the truth, but you will not believe me,
> I am the city where you will not stay,
> I am your wife, your child, but you will leave me,
> I am the God to whom you will not pray.

Let us name our vulnerable God and thank him for the sunshine and for his constant presence in our lives.

* * *

Holy ground 1

When the LORD saw that he had turned aside to see, God called to him out of the bush, 'Moses, Moses!' And he said,

> *'Here I am.'* Then he said, *'Come no closer! Remove the sandals from your feet, for the place on which you are standing is holy ground.'*

> Exodus 3.4–5

What and where is 'holy ground'? First, my guess is that most of us think of noble cathedrals or small, peaceful chapels, places where we have a sense of the presence of God, where honour is given to him and prayers are often said.

At one time I was privileged to live, as a member of a community, in a beautiful Tudor house which had its own exquisite chapel, the oratory, where people had been praying for centuries. Visitors sometimes commented, 'The fabric of this building is steeped in prayer.' Something made them feel that they stood on holy ground.

When my husband was very young, his school took the boys to Walsingham where they had to walk barefoot for a mile to the Shrine of Our Lady. Walsingham has been a place of pilgrimage to Mary since medieval times. Both Catholics and Anglicans have erected splendid buildings, ancient and modern, in her honour. But when I went there I made for two places where I knew I would experience a sense of God's presence. One was the richly ornate and colourful Greek Orthodox chapel, which had formerly been a railway station; the other was the tiny, very plain but beautiful chapel of the Little Sisters of Jesus.

I believe that this ground can be found in other places too, in homes where there is loving-kindness and where good people live, for God makes his home in people as well as in religious buildings. Wherever true courage, true compassion and true generosity are found, which may be in the street, in a hospital, in a prison, we can (metaphorically if not literally) take off our shoes in reverence and in acknowledgement that we are in the presence of something – someone – who fills us with awe.

* * *

Holy ground 2

My friend Michael, a Jesuit priest, was travelling in India when he was invited to visit the Golden Temple in Amritsar, which is the home of the Sikhs.

In a letter he wrote:

> My host showed me round the various buildings which make up the temple complex and then took me to the Golden Temple itself. Ornate and magnificently decorated as it was on the outside, I was surprised to find the actual sanctuary quite small and intimate. In the centre on a raised dais rests the Holy Book – the Guru Granth Sahib. In front musicians pound out devotional songs. In odd little corners sit devotees muttering from tiny pocket books or silently telling their rosary beads. Despite the crowds the atmosphere is still. I think I can honestly say that the Golden Temple is one of the most deeply spiritual places I have ever visited. The atmosphere of prayer is soaked into the golden plates which cover the building.

It sounds from Michael's description as though there was holy ground in the Golden Temple, as surely it is to be found in some synagogues, Friends' Meeting Houses, mosques and Free Church chapels. For the Holy Spirit 'bloweth where she listeth', and where the Holy Spirit dwells, there is holy ground.

Michael is a Roman Catholic priest, but most of his life has been spent studying, teaching and writing on inter-faith matters. This means that he has an intimate knowledge of many religions other than his own and has made many good friends among their followers. I think Michael would say that his own Christian faith has been strengthened and enriched by his experiences. I do not believe that any one faith can hold the whole truth; there are many paths to God and many riches to share.

* * *

Idleness

. . . they learn to be idle, gadding about from house to house, and they are not merely idle, but also gossips and busybodies.

1 Timothy 5.13

St Paul is giving Timothy instructions for leading the Christian community in Ephesus, and here is giving his rather severe opinion of what young widows are likely to get up to!

But I believe that there is something to be said for idleness. Tonight I am doing nothing, absolutely nothing. I am not gadding about or being a busybody; I am simply sitting quietly in my rocking chair by the fire.

It's true that I have had to fight off feelings of guilt. I could be defrosting the fridge or tidying the kitchen drawers or writing an overdue letter to a friend.

But I made a decision to do none of these things, and gradually the guilt ebbs away as I relax in the peacefulness of the room. And into my mind comes the picture of a field I once saw when I was out walking on the moors. It belonged to what was clearly a well-kept, flourishing farm. There were other fields around it, some with cattle, others with sheep, and also fields of ripening barley. But this one was quite empty as though the farmer had forgotten all about it.

I was puzzled until I realized that this was a field deliberately left fallow so that the soil could rest for a year and its nutrients be replenished. This way it would yield a richer harvest next time.

I'm not sure whether this idleness of mine today will be fruitful, but I hope so. Idleness is like emptiness. Jesus 'emptied himself, taking the form of a slave, being born in human likeness' (Philippians 2.7). And if we can empty ourselves of all the niggling, trivial distractions of our lives, just for a little while, in idleness, then perhaps we are giving 'whatever is true, whatever is pure, whatever is pleasing' within us a chance to see the light of day and grow.

* * *

Rest

So God blessed the seventh day and hallowed it, because on it God rested from all the work that he had done in creation.

Genesis 2.3

Remember the sabbath day, and keep it holy.
Exodus 20.8

Some people may tell you that they work 'twenty-four seven', by which they mean all day and every day. This is patently not true, because everyone has to sleep some of the time, even so-called workaholics; it is also a very bad idea.

If we want to fulfil our potential we will need to take a rest from time to time. Jesus knew this. His work of teaching and healing was exhausting, and sometimes he would make his escape. I am always touched by the scene in the Gospels where he is very tired and aware that his disciples are too. He says, 'Come away to a deserted place all by yourselves and rest a while' (Mark 6.31). But it was to no avail because the crowds were hungry for his presence and caught up with them.

Dorothy Day was an outstanding Christian of the twentieth century. She worked among the poorest in New York, with an open house, welcoming people who were alcoholic, or demented, or generally down-and-out, for over forty years. People were astounded by her hard work and unending commitment and generosity, but she told them she always took two days off a week, a recipe against burn-out.

For Christians, the day of rest is Sunday. It should be a time of refreshment, of letting go, and, at least in part, of quietness. Jesus had common sense: he was happy to let his disciples eat ears of corn on the Sabbath, and certain that it would be wrong not to cure the man with a withered hand just because it was the Sabbath. In the same way it is not necessary for us to keep Sunday so strictly that we don't allow ourselves any fun or pleasure on that day. 'The sabbath was made for humankind, not humankind for the sabbath,' said Jesus (Mark 2.27), and the same applies to Sunday, our Christian day of rest.

* * *

Responding to those in need 1

When he was near the gate of the town, there was a dead man being carried out, the only son of his mother, and she was a widow. And a considerable number of the towns-people was with her. When the Lord saw her he felt sorry for her, and said to her, 'Don't cry.' Then he went up and touched the bier and the bearers stood still, and he said, 'Young man, I tell you to get up.'

Luke 7.12, New Jerusalem Bible

In the Gospels we constantly read of people coming to Jesus to be cured. There are also times when it is he who takes the initiative. He chose to restore the woman's son to life, to cure the old woman who could not stand upright and the man with the withered hand. As far as we know, none of them asked for his help. Jesus had no need to seek out the disabled and infirm; they came to him in droves. Yet he did go spontaneously to help people in difficulty or distress.

But I, who live in comfort, warmth and plenty, do have a need to go out sometimes and try to befriend and help the marginalized, those who are 'on the edge', who have so much less. It's not enough to stay at home saying my prayers, think-ing holy thoughts and waiting for someone to turn up who would like my assistance.

* * *

Responding to those in need 2

I thought about this recently when I was in Budapest for a few days. In the guide book it describes the street I was walking down as 'alive with musicians and street entertainers' but, perhaps because it was November, there were only a few desultory shoppers to be seen.

Suddenly, I heard a strange moaning sound. I turned round to see an old woman striding along on huge crutches. She moved quite fast and had soon overtaken me, but not before I had seen that she was old and ill and somehow grotesque, carrying a small begging bowl in her twisted hand. From behind she looked even worse: both legs were in plaster and bandaged but her feet were bare. Blood was seeping through at her heels.

I felt shocked and sickened. Nobody was taking any notice of her, nobody gave her money. Soon she was out of sight but I couldn't forget her. An hour or so later I saw her again and slipped a few coins into her bowl. She murmured something, perhaps a blessing, and went on her way.

Later I told my Hungarian friend about the incident. She said that the woman was probably employed for a pittance by a Romanian gang-master, that the blood was probably fake and the whole act staged in order to con gullible foreigners like me.

However, I didn't regret giving the money because it seemed to me that her life was wretched enough whatever the truth.

It is always difficult to decide whether to give to people who beg. We are afraid that in giving money we may only be encouraging an addiction to alcohol or drugs, and at the same time we are tormented by the fear that we are being cruel in failing to stand in the shoes of someone so much worse off than ourselves. 'There but for the grace of God,' I say to myself, but . . . as the mother of an addicted son, I have no answer to this.

* * *

The sacredness of life

For you love all things that exist, and detest none of the things that you have made . . . you spare all things, for they are yours,

O Lord, you who love the living. For your immortal spirit is in all things.

The Wisdom of Solomon 11.24, 26; 12.1

God's Holy Spirit is not just in the sunset and the beautiful flowers, but even in the pebbles on the seashore. So all of life is sacred and deserves our reverence. It is because of this belief in the sanctity of life that many Christians are passionately opposed to abortion. They act under the pro-life banner, but often they look no further.

Since they believe that all life is sacred, why do they not campaign as fervently against capital punishment and against war? And why have they (and I include myself in this) been so long blind to the destruction of rain forests and coral reefs and the catastrophic extinction of so many species of animals, insects and birds?

When we begin to love creation as God loves it, then we will earnestly want to save our planet from ruin, ruin which is largely caused by the greed for money and power of those with business interests like logging that have such far-reaching and disastrous consequences.

If we are serious about being followers of Christ, then we will want to repent of our ignorance and indifference. We will want to live more simply. We will eat less meat, so that the world's hungry people, rather than beef cattle, can be fed. We will be concerned for the welfare and happiness of the generations to come, doing all in our power to leave them a world as fruitful and beautiful as the one we ourselves enjoy.

* * *

Doris

The souls of the righteous are in the hand of God . . .
and the faithful will abide with him in love
because grace and mercy are upon his holy ones.

The Wisdom of Solomon 3.1, 9

A great lady of our town has died this week. Her name was Doris, and she would have described herself as 'nowt but an ordinary working lass'.

Doris died at the age of 86 and only recently had to give up caring for the old folk (most of them younger than herself) who lived round her in the old part of town.

She was a bonny woman with an open smiling face and a laugh you could recognize from one end of the street to the other. Almost every time we met she would ask after the bairns, my children and grandchildren. It must have been a sadness that she and her late husband, Jack, never had children of their own. Although Doris never managed to get to their matches, she was a passionate supporter of Middlesbrough Football Club, for whom she lit thousands of candles over the years.

Doris was very devout, attending daily Mass when she could. At the sign of peace she would hug and kiss everyone around her, sometimes to the alarm of strangers. She was exuberant, noisy, happy and irrepressible. No menial task was too daunting for her, no favour too demanding.

Over the years I have had many conversations with Doris, but one stands out in my memory. A member of our congregation had been causing difficulties for others. She was arrogant and domineering. One day, after church, a group of us were criticizing her and agreeing that she was a disruptive influence in the parish. Suddenly Doris, who had been unusually quiet, spoke up. 'We don't know her sorrows,' she said.

Doris wasn't just a jolly, hard-working, selfless soul who laughed a lot; she was also wise and generous-hearted, a great lady.

* * *

Christian unity 1

The glory that you have given me I have given them, so that they may be one, as we are one, I in them and you in me, that they may become completely one, so that the world may know that you have sent me, and have loved them even as you have loved me.

John 17.22, 23

Will is a devout Roman Catholic who has lived all his life in the same village. One day he heard that the Anglicans were planning a Rogation Day procession and needed a cross. Without a word to anyone, Will looked out some pieces of wood and in his slow careful way fashioned a large cross.

When it was finished he looked at it with a craftsman's pleasure, noting the beauty of the grain and the soft sheen of the wood. But the cross was plain; there was no figure of Christ fixed to it like the one over Will's bed. He was about to go and buy a figure when something made him hesitate.

He remembered that Anglicans generally use plain crosses and thought his gift might be more generous if it didn't jar on their sensibilities. And as he held the cross in his hands and looked down on it, he thought about Christ crucified, and realized that because his imagination had free rein, the impact the bare cross had on him was far more striking than that of the crucifix he had at home. The suffering of Jesus grew more real to him as he gazed at the plain cross, the work of his own hands.

A week or two later the vicar came round to Will's cottage. 'We are delighted and grateful to receive the cross,' he said, and handed Will an envelope. 'We have collected some money towards your brother's work with the poor in India,' he added. Inside the envelope was a cheque for £50.

* * *

Christian unity 2

In Will's village, people were unselfconsciously moving towards Christian unity. A Roman Catholic made something for the Anglicans, and in response they gave him something towards the work of Catholics. Incidents like this were occurring frequently among the neighbours in this village, involving Methodists, Baptists, Quakers and members of the United Reformed Church. And in the case of Will something perhaps even more important happened. Thinking for himself and open to the values outside his own tradition, he had discovered a new approach to God which deepened his own spirituality.

Sometimes, at the annual service in Unity Week, a preacher will touch the hearts of the congregation and move some of them to do something about it. But I believe that the message has now been received, and taken to heart, that Christians want to be united and find that as far as working, praying and living go, our differences are negligible. Small gestures, small awakenings like Will's, are happening everywhere. Christians want Christianity to flourish and to be *seen* to flourish. They want to befriend and learn from one another and work together for justice, serving the disadvantaged in their communities. They may sympathize with the scholars and experts who struggle to find a way forward doctrinally, but all the while, slowly and quietly, the movement towards unity is gaining momentum. The theologians may be frustrated and near to despair, but the people of God are getting on with it. It is those at the grass roots that are growing into the green shoots of hope.

* * *

Water

For waters shall break forth in the wilderness,
and streams in the desert;
the burning sand shall become a pool,
and the thirsty ground springs of water.
Isaiah 35.6–7

A good friend of mine, who had been working hard for months to make her church fête a success, called at my house the day before the event was due to take place in the Rectory garden.

'Please pray that it won't rain tomorrow!' she said.

But I didn't pray that it wouldn't rain. I wanted my friend to be happy, I hoped the sun would be shining on the Rectory garden next day, I knew the purpose of the fête was to raise money for a good cause, but my prayers were for something different: I was praying for those who so desperately *needed* rain. I knew that in Africa thousands of people, adults and their children, were starving and dying because the rains had failed.

All life on land is ultimately dependent on fresh water, and the sole source of fresh water is rain. Plants, animals and humans alike die when there is not enough water to sustain them. Scientists say that because of humanity's greed and wanton destruction, the supply of water on our planet is rapidly diminishing. They predict that by the end of this century one quarter of the continent of Africa will be so severely short of water that millions of 'water refugees' will flee to Northern Europe.

Jesus said: 'Those who drink of the water that I will give them will never be thirsty' (John 4.14). Just as water is the source of life on earth, so Jesus is the source of life with God for those who follow his teaching.

And incidentally, I am happy to record that although it rained heavily on the day of the fête, a record sum of money was raised for the good cause!

* * *

The perfect wife

A capable wife who can find?
She is far more precious than jewels.
The heart of her husband trusts in her,
and he will have no lack of gain . . .
She seeks wool and flax
and works with willing hands . . .
She rises while it is still night

and provides food for her household . . .
she puts her hands to the distaff,
and her hands hold the spindle.
                    Proverbs 31.10, 11, 13, 15, 19

I have quoted only a few of the attributes of this paragon of a wife. Alas, I compare very unfavourably with such a splendid woman, who runs her household so efficiently and has all the skills of a fine seamstress. I can sew on a button and make a stab at darning a hole in a sock, but that's about it. My gifts are different, and so is my attitude to my husband. I try to make him happy, but I don't put him on a pedestal. Nor would he want to be there.

Which brings me to St Paul, writing to the Colossians:

Wives, be subject to your husbands, as is fitting in the Lord.
Husbands, love your wives and never treat them harshly.
                    Colossians 3.18, 19

The feminist in me sees red when I read this, but the weaker? wiser? part of me thinks that (a) Paul was a man of his own time, and (b) if a husband truly loves his wife and is never harsh with her, then perhaps there is no hardship in being subject to him.

And Paul himself, in his letter to the Galatians, writes: 'There is no longer Jew or Greek, there is no longer slave or free, there is no longer male and female; for all of you are one in Christ Jesus' (Galatians 3.28).

* * *

Wildest dreams 1

The LORD said to Abraham, 'Why did Sarah laugh, and say, "Shall I indeed bear a child, now that I am old?" Is anything too wonderful for the LORD? At the set time, I will return to you, in due season, and Sarah shall have a son.'
                    Genesis 18.13–14

Now Sarah said, 'God has brought laughter for me; every-
one who hears will laugh with me.' And she said, 'Who would
ever have said to Abraham that Sarah would nurse children?
Yet I have borne him a son in his old age.'

Genesis 21.6–7

At the age of 99, not in her wildest dreams did Sarah believe
that she would bear a child, but it happened. This was a rare
phenomenon; such dreams don't often come true because they
are too wild, too crazy or too impossible.

I first met Joan at one of the special services our church puts
on every year for those with learning difficulties. She was with
her son, Matthew, who obviously had a lot of problems and
seemed distressed. But Joan said, 'Matt loves this day. He looks
forward to it for months.'

Some years later I met Joan again, this time in our doctor's
surgery. She looked a lot older. Her face was lined and pale and
her hands were trembling. She said, 'I'm so worried. My health
is really deteriorating and I don't know if I can manage looking after Matt much longer.' She was trying not to cry.

'Is there somewhere he could go?' I asked.

'No,' she said, with a big sigh. 'Social Services showed us round
two or three places but they were all so big and drab and cheer-
less and Matt hated them. What am I to do?'

* * *

Wildest dreams 2

'I don't know, Joan,' I said, 'but I'll see if I can find something
out for you.' Two weeks later I drove Joan and Matt to a little
house in a back street near the town centre. Inside it was bright
and clean. My friend Rosemary welcomed us, smiling at all three
of us. 'I'm the warden here,' she said. 'We only have places for
four people, but there's a vacancy, and you could have that place,
Matthew, if you'd like it.' According to Joan, Matthew would like
it, very much.

Later I asked Joan how she felt about the house as home for Matt. 'It's wonderful,' she said, 'it's beyond my wildest dreams.' I felt like weeping.

Joan had spent forty or so years in devoted care of her son, forty years without a holiday, forty years of facing other people's non-acceptance. And her wildest dreams were nothing like mine, which were of adventure and excitement and success and beauty and a reciprocal loving relationship. I wondered about the quality of her life, about her fulfilment of herself as a person, about her friendships and fun. I could only imagine. And as I thought and wondered, I began to see her in a different light. In my mind I looked at her not with pity, but with admiration and a feeling of humility.

I was suddenly aware of the limitedness of my loving, for hers was without limit. And I could see that it was her life, not mine, that was rich, a life not of dreams but of reality, a life not of rewards but of great cost. I know that in her selfless loving, the Spirit must surely be working.

* * *

The cross

So they took Jesus; and carrying the cross by himself, he went out to what is called The Place of the Skull.

John 19.16–17

I have several crucifixes and crosses in my house, all of which I value because of their associations. The biggest, and arguably the most beautiful of them, hangs in our bedroom. My husband and I gave it to each other when we were married, and it was made by a Polish sculptor at the Carmelite friary in Aylesford, Kent. The bronze figure of Christ is graceful and he looks benign rather than tortured. Also on our bedroom wall is a tiny fragile crucifix, made and sold in Rwanda in aid of the victims of genocide. It is not a work of art, but it is evocative of suffering, and it was a gracious gift from a friend.

In our living room there are two crosses. One is a copy of an ancient carving of Christ the King. I like it very much but it is comical and charming rather than spiritually challenging. The other is a small plain cross of beaten bronze. We bought it in France after a very happy holiday, and we chose it because it is not symmetrical, and in this simple fact seems to symbolize for us the vulnerability of Jesus.

Put away in a drawer are two very special crosses. A young German girl, who had lived with us in a Christian community and from the day she arrived had cheerfully mocked our faith, thrust a clumsily wrapped parcel into my hands in the very last minute before she went through the gate to catch her plane home. Inside were two twigs bound together with rough string in the shape of a cross. This cross stays in the drawer because it would fall apart anywhere else, but it is a treasure. The smallest crucifix stays in the drawer because it is not big enough to fix on the wall. Our teenage adopted son, who had previously tried to trash most of our religious objects and symbols, surreptitiously slipped it under the duvet when I was ill in bed. It certainly is not beautiful, but it certainly *is* precious.

* * *

Darkness

Even if I go through the deepest darkness
I will not be afraid, Lord, for you are with me.
Psalm 23.4, Good News Bible

Sometimes I long for darkness: no light pollution, no stars, no moon, no sun; just complete darkness enveloping me, I who love the brightness of noonday, the gentler light of winter and the cold mysterious lovely light of the moon. Still, I need darkness.

Sometimes I long for silence: no music, no traffic, no shouting, just silence enfolding me, I who love the pure voices of choirboys, the song of blackbirds, the lapping of waves and the howling of gales. Still, I long for silence.

Sometimes I long for emptiness: no pressure, no parties, no demands, just the nothing of emptiness baring my soul, I who love challenges, fulfilment and feasts.

I don't think I'm unusual in this. Many of us are attracted in opposing directions, pulled in two ways. But some people give their whole lives to solitude and silence: contemplative nuns and hermits seeking the solitary life. Those who seek to live in this way, spending their days as entirely as is possible in contemplation of God, are not cutting themselves off from people; rather, they become more and more receptive to those who approach them seeking healing or wisdom or prayer. Meister Eckhart said, 'What we receive in contemplation, we give out in love.'

This is certainly true of the Poor Clares, enclosed nuns who give their lives to prayer and receive requests for prayer from people in every kind of distress. Their knowledge of what goes on in the world and behind closed doors is often more extensive than that of most of us.

But such a life is not mine. My dream of darkness, silence and solitude and emptiness will probably never be fulfilled, but I will keep on dreaming.

* * *

Peace with justice 1

> *In his days justice shall flourish*
> *and peace till the moon fails.*
> Psalm 72.7, Grail Psalms

Variations on peace

> Everyone said, 'Martin, you need a break.'
> He had been out to Sri Lanka
> comforting survivors and helping to rebuild homes
>   after the tsunami.
> Back in London he worked day and night
> supporting asylum seekers till everyone said,

'Martin, you need a break.'
So he went away to a cottage in the country.
He lay in bed admiring the starry sky,
listening to the silence.
'This is wonderful,' he murmured, 'this is peace.'
And he slept the sleep of the just.

Next morning Martin awoke.
He smiled, and lazily stretched,
'Peace, perfect peace,' he said.
Then he switched on the radio
and heard about the earthquake in Kashmir.
'No peace for the wicked,' he said.
'Martin, you needed some peace,'
his wife and his colleagues sighed
when he left to board a plane for Kashmir.
Martin grinned and said, 'There is no peace,
not without justice.'

* * *

Peace with justice 2

The cheerful ballad about Martin promotes a truth. As follow-ers of Christ we cannot sit back and do nothing when the world is in such turmoil. It is a mistake to think that true peace is a sort of lazy contentment, that it means shunning the world and all its problems, concentrating instead on the comfort and welfare of 'number one'.

The Hebrew word which in the Bible is translated as 'peace' is *shalom*. It has a far richer content than our word, meaning a condition of happiness and wholeness in which we are in right relationship with God and also with our fellow men and women. It follows that there can be no peace without justice. Ironically, we will never have peace unless we fight for justice, not with guns, but with voices raised on behalf of the poor, the hungry, the oppressed, the dispossessed, the victims of power-seeking and greed.

The worst enemies of peace are those who, in pursuit of money or power, make and sell arms to countries where, as a result, thousands of innocent civilians are maimed or killed in warfare. And the best friends of peace are those who become involved in the struggle for justice on behalf of their brothers and sisters who suffer in consequence of our inhumanity.

Clearly, and just as well, we can't all be like Martin, rushing to the aid of everyone in need both at home and abroad, but we can try to discern God's will for us and seek ways in which we can further the cause of justice. Jesus did not say, 'Blessed are those who are at peace,' he said, 'Blessed are the *peacemakers*,' and the next beatitude is: 'Blessed are those who are persecuted for the sake of justice' (Matthew 5.9–10, my translation).

* * *

Worship

Worship the LORD in the beauty of holiness.
1 Chronicles 16.29, Authorized Version

Trying to worship the Lord in the beauty of holiness is exactly what this book is about.

Recently I was in a congregation of Christians from different traditions who were questioning John Sentamu, the Archbishop of York, about his faith. Someone asked him, 'What are the two most important elements in your spiritual life?' He answered without hesitation, 'Worship and witness.'

By worship, he told us, he did not mean saying prayers and singing hymns of adoration, but doing the will of God and, as far as we can, living Christ-like lives.

We can do this in quietness and humility, not wanting to draw attention to any progress we might make in virtue. And we can also be witnesses for Christ, letting our light shine so that others might be attracted to follow him. To achieve this balance, we need to live in holiness, and to dedicate our whole lives to God in love.

We worship God because of our love for him and because of his great love for us, answering to the wonder and beauty of his creation, responding to each person we encounter in our lives as our brothers and sisters, beloved children of our Father.

As the writer of Psalm 95 said:

> O come, let us worship and bow down,
> let us kneel before the LORD our Maker!
> For he is our God,
> and we are the people of his pasture,
> and the sheep of his hand.
>
> Psalm 95.6, 7

* * *

Shining star

Do all things without murmuring and arguing, so that you may be blameless and innocent, children of God without blemish in the midst of a crooked and perverse generation, in which you shine like stars in the world.

Philippians 2.14–15

I think of Sally-Anne when I read this passage, because as a child in the school where I taught, she could do nothing without murmuring (or rather, muttering under her breath) and arguing. And that was on a good day. More often than not, she was shouting and swearing, and when it came to fighting she was tougher than any of the boys.

Exasperated and infuriated as we were, the staff would make excuses for Sally-Anne. We knew she came from a very poor family, and although her mother had never managed to turn up for open evenings or school events, we knew she was a lone parent. As soon as she was 16, Sally-Anne left school, and I have to admit that I was among those who felt relieved, not to say glad.

I didn't see her again until about eight years later, when I bumped into her in the street. She hailed me enthusiastically, and at first I didn't recognize her. She seemed so pleased to see me that I invited her to come for a coffee.

Sally-Anne talked, and I listened, gradually feeling more and more ashamed. I hadn't really known her as a child at all, but now the reasons for her behaviour became only too apparent. From the age of four she had been sexually abused by her father. He left home when she was 11, and by the time she was 12 her brother had begun the same abuse. At 18 she had been diagnosed with epilepsy and diabetes and pronounced unfit for work.

So why, I wondered, had she changed so much? I remembered her constant frowns and sulky mouth and outrageous clothes. Now she looked a bit shabby, but clean and happy. She apologized again for her behaviour at school.

Then she told me, 'I'm a Christian now. I work every day with my church, some days with the homeless, and some with druggies. I love it! I love them!'

Then she grinned. 'You never thought I would turn out like this, did you, Miss?'

I laughed and said, 'You're a star, Sally-Anne.'

* * *

Small groups

For where two or three are gathered in my name, I am there among them.

Matthew 18.20

In the name of Jesus I used to meet regularly with five other women. To begin with we were not all friends. I knew Mary only a little and I hadn't met Norah before. We came from different social and educational backgrounds, and different Christian traditions. What we had in common was the desire to pray together.

Not very much was said. We took it in turns to start the prayer time with some Scripture, a poem or particular idea, and then we spent the rest of the time in silence. For me, and I think for all the others, it felt like a deeply spiritual experience, both peaceful and refreshing.

On one level, nothing happened. I think my own spiritual awareness increased, but what grew and flowered unexpectedly was the growth of trust and love among us. At the end of the silence, a prayer was spoken, and then we talked about our most pressing concerns, so that little by little we came to know one another at greater depth. It was a hallowed time in the week, and is a memory I treasure.

I know that there are some parishes where similar small groups flourish. This seems to me to be a promising way forward, especially as congregations are dwindling and getting older. Such groups can be a forum for new people to relax together, to feel included, to share their concerns, to grow in love of God and one another and to develop an understanding of their part in building community.

Too many people come to church alone, take part in the service and silently slip away afterwards. They are a living part of the body of Christ, but no-one knows their name or circumstances. Invite them to a small unthreatening group which gathers in the name of Jesus, and their lives may be transformed.

* * *

The brokenhearted

The LORD is near to the brokenhearted,
and saves the crushed in spirit.
Psalm 34.18

Where is your God? Where is your God now? Why didn't he prevent this? Why doesn't he intervene to save her from dying?

These are the questions that spring from the anguish of a broken heart. I cannot pretend to have an answer or an explanation. The problem of suffering and the problem of evil have been agonized over by theologians and philosophers for centuries, but still the answer is the same: 'We don't know.'

People are understandably puzzled and legitimately angry when they ask: 'If God is all-loving and all-powerful, how could he have allowed all those innocent children to be smothered to death under a mud slide?' 'Why doesn't he intervene to save the life of my husband?'

I do not share this understanding of God, because I believe that his only power is the power of love. And I believe most passionately that he is not only close to us when our hearts are broken, but equally present to us when we cry out in terrible anger against him. Then he is like a mother firmly holding on to her screaming child, loving him through his tantrum until his rage at last subsides.

Ten years after the shooting at Dunblane, where so many young children were needlessly killed, I heard the Revd Colin McIntosh, the minister at Dunblane Cathedral, comparing God's love to the love of a parent, and saying that the time comes when, however reluctantly, we have to let our grown-up children go out into the world with the freedom to take risks and make mistakes. We don't have control over them any more, but whatever happens we continue to love them.

So it is with God. He does not curtail our freedom, but his is the love that will not let us go, so he remains forever close to those whose hearts are broken.

* * *

Waiting

> *It is good that one should wait quietly*
> *for the salvation of the LORD.*
> Lamentations 3.26

The grandmother I knew best and loved the most we called Granny. She always wore black with a tiny white frill round the neck and I never saw her ankles, let alone her legs.

Why did I love her? Perhaps most of all because she was always there. She didn't travel; I don't ever remember her going out. In my memory she is always sitting in the same chair: dignified, wise, sparkling with humour.

Now I am a grandmother. My grandchildren call me Anth. I wear jeans; in summer my feet are sandalled, my legs bare. I travel around the world and I am afraid I am not particularly dignified. Wise? I don't feel wise although my experience of life must be so much more intense than Granny's ever was.

It is different now, especially this time as I wait for my fourth grandchild, who will be a little girl. Becky, Jake and Luke were born when I was still working, still swept along in an exhausting whirl of activity and people and events. I wait for Susannah? Megan? in stillness, my thoughts and prayers and dreams revolving around her. I seem to love her already, to know the blessing she is, and smile because she is late, keeping us waiting, in no hurry to leave the security of that safe place.

What gift shall I give to someone who will herself be so precious a gift? I am waiting till I see her. There are a thousand questions I could ask: is she destined to be happy? intelligent? beautiful? handicapped in some way? Even, is she destined to live? But I am not asking these questions. I am simply glad to wait, slowly pondering on all the mysteries of hope and birth and life and love, quietly rejoicing in my renewed sense of wonder.

* * *

Judgement

Do not judge, so that you may not be judged.
Matthew 7.1

On the television news I saw a dear little old lady of 97 with her face badly bruised and beaten. Four young thugs had broken into her home, taken her money, tied and gagged her and threatened to kill her.

What was my reaction as I sat and watched? The same as everyone else's, I imagine. How horrible! How disgusting! How can human beings behave with such brutality? I hope they are caught and made to suffer! I was angry, and I was out for vengeance.

Only when the shock and indignation had evaporated a little did I begin to try to think as a Christian. I was still angry, but I was directing my anger not against the young men, but at the dreadful thing they had done. I still wanted them caught and punished, but most of all I thought they should be helped to understand the enormity of their action.

I don't think being a Christian necessarily means being 'soft'; sometimes it means just the opposite. I am not going to excuse those thugs from all guilt because they had unhappy childhoods. I know a number of people who had deprived and miserable childhoods and have grown up to be compassionate and caring adults.

But at the same time, I believe it is vital to recognize that freedom is very relative. If you are born into a loving family and inherit intelligence and a happy personality, if you have enough money to live comfortably, good health and pleasant surroundings, and most of all if you are confident of God's love for you, then you are free indeed, free to live in imitation of Christ. For many people, the opposite is true. They grow up without the experience of being loved. They do not know about God or Jesus Christ. In their world, selfishness and cruelty are not only acceptable but normal.

I think I have to ask myself: 'Who am I, to make judgements on anyone?'

* * *

The reality of love

[Love] bears all things, believes all things, hopes all things, endures all things.

1 Corinthians 13.7

Christ was 'for real'. When God became man he was as naked and helpless and vulnerable as a human can be – a newborn child needing food and clothing and above all love, growing up to need sunshine and beauty and freedom and fun.

We are often told that the stable and manger signify poverty, but I think the Incarnation, God's becoming human, has a still deeper significance. Jesus represents and identifies with the poor, but beyond that he is at the heart of reality, at the heart of what life and people and relationships are all about.

That is why when Christ asks us to love one another he is not talking about something cosy, self-satisfying, exclusive. He is talking about the encounter between people at a level of reality. Romantic love, sexual love, dependent love, possessive love . . . none of these, though they may bring pleasure, happiness and comfort, come to grips with what it means to relate to another person in the reality of love. That only happens when we accept someone totally, when you and I stand naked before each other in the sense of being stripped of all pretence, and still glad to embrace.

We are so cluttered up with fears, inhibitions, prejudices, frustrations and resentments that it takes a frightening amount of courage and patience to cut through to our own centre, let alone expose it to anyone else. Fear, in its various forms, is surely the greatest barrier to love. No wonder Jesus kept on saying, 'Do not be afraid.'

In the church, too, we are cluttered up with inessentials. We are urged to save our own souls by careful observance of the law, and when we are exhorted to love our neighbour it is seldom explained what that means in depth. The burning issues of our world today, peace, justice and deprivations, are not often spoken of with passion from the pulpit. Sadly, being a practising Christian can sometimes mean more of an escape from reality into being a 'good', conforming person, than a commitment to what love and life are all about.

* * *

Commitment

Into your hand I commit my spirit;
you have redeemed me, O Lord, faithful God.
Psalm 31.5

A lukewarm Christian is a contradiction in terms: there is
no such animal. If we really believe in Jesus Christ and the
message of love that he brings, then we have to be totally
committed to him and continually trying to live out the good
news of the gospel. Going to church on Sunday, fulfilling
our 'obligations', just isn't enough – it's hardly worth anything
at all if it's done as a duty. Who, knowing Christ, could
imagine that he wanted us to be 'obliged' to do anything in
his name?

He came, the Way, the Truth and the Life, to show us how
to live, to teach us how to love.

He asks for nothing, yet he demands everything. To be a
Christian is to belong to Christ, and to belong to Christ means
to imitate him. So I must live my whole life with him as my
centre, not just my churchgoing and my prayers: my work, my
pleasure, my rest, my grief and my joy.

How to do this? It's difficult at first, because for most of us
it means a turn-about, a re-orientation of our thinking – in other
words, a conversion: perhaps for Christians a conversion from
being only 'Sunday Christians' to being real Christians the other
six days as well.

And yet, in a sense, it's easy too. What it needs is willingness, most of all the willingness to be open to God and his
love. Once we've taken that step, the rest will follow, slowly,
perhaps, but surely. Being open to God, we will want to
pray: the sort of praying that is not 'saying prayers', but
giving our time to be still with him and receive what he has
to give.

Gradually we will begin to see our way more clearly and to
understand that this is what our life is all about, that when
we pray to him God will respond by loving through us, and we,

the people of God, will become new people, living in love and
longing ever to grow in love.

Mass at The Spike

The spirit of the Lord GOD is upon me . . .
he has sent me to bring good news to the oppressed,
to bind up the broken-hearted,
to proclaim liberty to the captives,
and release to the prisoners.

Isaiah 61.1

The Spike in Southampton was a reception centre for ex-
prisoners and down-and-outs and alcoholics. One Sunday I went
there to Mass.

There was nothing beautiful to see
in honour of the Lord,
the readings were badly done, the responses feeble,
there was hardly any sermon . . .
At Mass, the priest identifies with Christ,
breaking the bread and saying,
'This is my body.'
Sometimes it is hard, watching and listening
to imagine Christ.
But today, at The Spike, it was different.
The priest in this Mass was striving
to identify with Christ in another way,
to reach the men who were there
and loving them, to be one of them.
The Lord is close to the brokenhearted.
Their hearts were touched, and so was mine,
I was glad and very blessed to have been there.

Mairi's Good Friday 1

When Jesus had received the wine, he said, 'It is finished.'
Then he bowed his head and gave up his spirit.

John 19.30

Today, Good Friday, life on earth was finished for Mairi too when she gave up her spirit and died tragically, two doors away from us. She lived alone, and in the early hours of this morning her house was set on fire by causes yet unknown. All the neighbours came out, at first trying to rescue Mairi, but forced back by the power of smoke and flames. Then two of the men climbed a ladder and tried to put out the fire with a hose . . . the fire engine took maybe ten minutes to arrive, but of course it seemed like hours to us who were waiting. For me, the worst moment was when I heard a frantic cry of 'Mairi!' from a neighbour, desperately hoping she would come to the window.

There isn't really a valid comparison with the death of Jesus. The police told us that Mairi must have been in a deep sleep and would not have suffered at all. Nor was she sacrificing herself for others. But there was one similarity between the two Good Friday deaths, and that was the human response.

All the neighbours had gathered outside, some in their nightclothes. Looking at them from across the way, I saw that they were huddled in a silent tableau, some weeping, some with a comforting arm thrown round another's shoulders, but all of them still, all gazing upwards to Mairi's window, surely much as Mary and the others must have gazed up at Christ on his cross, with the same intensity, the same mixture of helplessness and disbelief.

It was a sorrowful beginning to a sorrowful day.

* * *

Mairi's Good Friday 2

It is still Good Friday and I have come home from the Walk of Witness which the churches organize together each year in our town. As I joined in the hymns and prayers and listened to the meditations, I became aware that I was thinking more about Mairi, who had died in the night, than about Jesus himself. This was my human weakness and I felt certain that God would understand.

At this time of year, our communal garden, which is tended by Mairi and others of the neighbours who love gardening, is at the peak of its loveliness. It is not so much that everything is neat and tidy, and there is not a weed to be discovered. Rather, the beauty of the garden lies in the delicate perfection of each spring flower: anemones, cowslips, primroses.

I am not one of the gardeners, but when I stepped out of my door this morning I was shocked and dismayed to find a torn and trampled flower lying across my path. It was just one crumpled scarlet petal, and I think it was a small tulip. It seemed all wrong that, in such a place, something once so beautiful was now lifeless and broken.

At once I thought, 'This is Mairi, broken, once beautiful, now lifeless Mairi!' and I couldn't bring myself to throw it away. I left it there, untidy on the path.

Mairi loved colour. She had painted her front door scarlet, and also the old chair where she sometimes used to sit on summer afternoons. She told us stories of her childhood on the Isle of Lewis, in the Hebrides. Her granny used to dye fabric from the wild plants that grew near her home, and as a little girl Mairi watched with delight as Granny pegged different coloured cloths in a row on the washing line. Their brilliance was the inspiration for her career as a fabric designer.

Mairi is dead now, the tulip is dead, Jesus is dead. But the green blade will rise again and the memory of Mairi will live.

* * *

Beauty 1

> *I will be like the dew to Israel;*
> *he shall blossom like the lily . . .*

his beauty shall be like the olive tree,
and his fragrance like that of Lebanon.

Hosea 14.5, 6

I believe the adage that beauty is 'in the eye of the beholder', and something I experienced in India several years ago confirmed this for me.

I had my first baby in a hospital where he was the first white baby to be born. I know Sam will forgive me when I admit that in the first moments of seeing him I thought he was rather ugly. He had no hair at all; his nose was squashed and red as a tomato, and he was covered all over in a slimy-looking yellowish substance like the stuff ewes lick off their newborn lambs.

He looked a bit better after he had been cleaned up, but I was surprised when, only a short time after his birth, a stream of Malayali women came in and out of my room to look at the baby. Many of them had already had their babies, and before I went into labour I had seen some of them. Their skin was the colour of chocolate, sometimes milk chocolate, sometimes plain. Their hair was black, thick and shiny, often curly, but it was their liquid brown eyes that most held my attention. To me, each one of these babies was stunningly beautiful.

I lay in my bed, scarcely believing my eyes as the procession of women kept coming. They hardly glanced at me, but without exception they gazed adoringly down at little Sam in his cot, clasping their hands together to greet him and murmuring *nalla*, the Malayalam for 'beautiful'!

To me it is clear from this that beauty is a subjective concept. But I also believe that real beauty has little to do with physical attractiveness, and everything to do with loveliness and integrity within.

As for Sam, he is grown up now, and hardly good-looking, but in my judgement he is one of the 'good guys'.

* * *

Beauty 2

There is an Old Testament proverb which says, 'Charm is deceitful, and beauty is vain, but a woman who fears the LORD is to be praised' (Proverbs 31.30).

Nowadays in our western culture, certain men and women are known as 'the beautiful people'. They are the ones who have attained celebrity and are admired by surely gullible folk. The beautiful people are almost without exception successful, young, slim and rich. Many of them, in order to maintain their celebrity status, have undergone cosmetic surgery. Their faces may be 'perfect' but they often look vapid and characterless.

Some time ago the BBC produced some programmes called *Facing the Truth*. The idea came from the Truth and Reconciliation meetings in South Africa, but these sessions took place in Northern Ireland, and were overseen by Archbishop Tutu. The perpetrators and the victims of violence encountered one another in a courageous move towards reconciliation and healing. In one of the programmes, Desmond Tutu listened to the conversations between an apparently big bruiser of a man who admitted he had killed deliberately, for the sole reason that his victim was a Catholic, and the still-grieving family of a young man who had been murdered just because of his religious affiliation.

As the meeting drew to a close, the archbishop, obviously near to tears, thanked the participants for coming, and looking at them with gentle compassion said wonderingly, 'I think it is beautiful.'

Healing and reconciliation, often hard-won, are always beautiful, as are generosity, humility and truth. Of course, this sort of beauty cannot be perceived by our eyes, only by a response of the heart.

St Augustine thought God himself was beauty. 'Late have I loved thee, O Beauty so ancient and so new; yes, late have I loved thee. And behold, thou wert within me, and I out of myself where I was seeking thee.'

* * *

Iris

O LORD, how manifold are your works!
In wisdom you have made them all.

Psalm 104.24

This psalm is a great song of praise for all the wonders God has created. Sometimes something happens which jogs our awareness of the glory and magnificence of creation and makes us stand still in awe: the sudden appearance of a kingfisher in its brilliant plumage, or the unbounded joy in a skylark's song.

Today I was uplifted by an unexpected revelation. It was a dismal day, very cold and dark outside. My husband brought in a single flower – I thought it was a crocus – and put it in a glass and set it on the mantelpiece. I was surprised, because he usually prefers to leave flowers growing in the garden, and I didn't understand why he had brought in just one not especially interesting bloom. I assumed it had been accidentally broken by the gales.

We sat on either side of the fire for a while, reading. Suddenly my husband said, 'Look!' and pointed at the flower. I stared, entranced. The flower, not a crocus but a tiny delicate iris, was opening in front of my eyes. I couldn't believe what I was seeing as, slowly, steadily, the petals unfurled in the warmth from the fire, and the lovely face of the flower was revealed.

I was reflecting later on the transforming effect of the warmth on the bud of this iris, when the image of Craig flashed into my mind. Craig is 18 and he has Asperger's syndrome, which is a form of autism. All his young life his condition has caused him to withdraw from society and shun the company of other children and adults, until the steady, unthreatening friendliness of an Asian shopkeeper at the local corner shop, offered day after day to the silent boy, at length began to gain a response. In the warmth of Mr Patel's gentle concern Craig began to open up, to engage in conversation and to grow in confidence.

The iris and Craig, two small miracles among all the amazing wonders of the world our God has made.

* * *

Planet Earth

The earth is full of your creatures.
Yonder is the sea, great and wide,
creeping things innumerable are there,
living things both small and great.
                    Psalm 104.24–25

It has been a great treat, enjoyed by millions of people, to watch a television programme presented by David Attenborough and called *Planet Earth*.

In our everyday lives, if we keep our senses alert, we can find different manifestations of the glory of God's creation. To mention just a few: the majesty of an oak tree, the silvery gleam of rivers in sunshine, the quirky charm of ducks and swans and seabirds, the joyous song of birds in parks and woodland, the sweetness of apple and cherry blossom. Such delights are fairly common to us who live in Western Europe, even if our homes are in cities.

Other folk, people with money and a sense of adventure, travel the world to experience all kinds of rare animal species, as well as the highest mountains, the longest rivers, the deepest lakes and everything unusual.

But *Planet Earth* was unique as it brought into our homes sights and sounds of the remotest parts of the earth, sights and sounds beyond our imagining. It was an opportunity to enjoy the wonders of creation as we would never have thought possible.

The Holy Spirit inhabits the whole cosmos and gives breath to all life. We live in a sacred world where we are in relationship with every plant and creature of Nature. Therefore it is not enough to worship God in creation; we creatures owe it to him to preserve and protect the beautiful, magical world he has made.

* * *

Perfection 1

. . . set no bounds to your love.

Matthew 5.48, New Jerusalem Bible

A friend offered to show me his workshop. He is a maker and repairer of musical instruments, and I was full of admiration for the delicacy and precision of his work. Afterwards I said to him, 'It was lovely to see such perfection.'

'Ah, but there's no perfection in my work,' he said, and went on to tell me how the craftsmen who carved the stone in our ancient and beautiful cathedrals always made a tiny deliberate mistake in their work, because only God is perfect. And similarly, the Persian carpet weavers of old, who made such exquisite patterns, always dropped or broke a thread or two because only Allah is perfect.

I know quite a lot of good Christian people who are perfectionists. They do their utmost not to break any commandments, great or small, they strive never to tell a lie, never to say an unkind word about anyone, never to miss saying their prayers – in other words, never to put a Christian foot wrong.

I feel uneasy about this emphasis on perfection. I respect and admire people who are so determined to do everything right, but I believe that God is asking less and yet more than this. He asks less, in that he does not want us to be obsessed with continually striving to be good; he asks more, in that he wants us to stop keeping such a close watch on our own behaviour and instead open our minds and hearts in response to him and to whatever is happening around us.

But, and there is a but, Matthew tells us that Jesus said, 'Be perfect, therefore, as your heavenly Father is perfect' (Matthew 5.48). This troubled me for a long time because it did not seem to be in accord with the rest of Christ's teaching. I wondered if perhaps the word 'perfect' was not an exact translation of the original text. I looked at five of the six Bibles in my house, and each translation used the word 'perfect'. Near to giving up, I looked at the New Jerusalem Bible, and there, to my relief, I found these words, 'You must therefore set no bounds to your love, just as your heavenly father sets none to his.'

I have no hopes of being perfect; I can at least try to set no bounds to my love.

* * *

Perfection 2

Once upon a time there was a man named George. George was a perfectionist; he always had been. He married Judith, and her sunny, carefree personality was a good foil to his obsession with perfection. George was determined from the first to be a perfect husband. He wasn't, but he did succeed in making Judith very happy. Then, three years into his marriage, a daughter, Tessa, was born. George was determined to be a perfect father. He wasn't, but Tessa grew up healthy and happy and she loved both her parents dearly. George retired as a senior partner in his firm. He could look back on a wonderfully fulfilling life. He had only one real sorrow, and that he kept a secret: he was deeply disappointed not to have produced a son. But shortly after George retired, things began to go wrong. First, Tessa brought a young man home and announced that after she married him they were going to live in Australia. A year later, Judith died. It was very hard for George; without both Judith and Tessa, he felt desperately lonely. A friend advised him to take up a hobby, and he decided on gardening. News came from Australia that Tessa had given birth to a son, Joseph. George was ecstatic: a grandson in place of the son he never had! Meanwhile, he was making a perfect garden. Everything about it was perfect: flowers, shrubs, pond, orchard and patio. There was never a weed or a dead flower to be seen. But George's pride and joy was his lawn. It was absolutely perfect and admired by all passersby. Then, when Joey was four, his parents brought him to England. George couldn't hold back tears of joy when he saw him. He was everything he had dreamed of in a little boy. Two days later, when George got up and looked out of his window, he was momentarily overwhelmed by shock and horror. Young Joey was running around with a football on the LAWN! George just stood there and waited while he felt his anger and dismay subside, and a new understanding of himself slowly came into being. What sort of man was he? What sort of grandfather? No lawn, no garden, nothing at all mattered compared with the wonder of Joey. Quickly, George pulled on an old pair of shoes and rushed out to kick the ball with his grandson.

* * *

Clothing 1

> . . . clothe yourselves with compassion, kindness, humility, meekness and patience. Bear with one another . . . just as the Lord has forgiven you, so you also must forgive. Above all, clothe yourselves with love, which binds everything together in perfect harmony.
>
> Colossians 3.12–14

Perhaps Paul chose clothing as an image because it is what lies nearest to our bodies and hearts. It is what we wear every day of our lives and it is essential to our well-being (though naturists might not agree). As a Christian I need the clothing of love and humility; as a human being I sometimes need the warmth of an overcoat.

And clothing can be significant in other ways. Our appearance says something about us which may be quite superficial or meaningless, although it is usually, though not always, possible to tell the very rich from the very poor by their clothing. There is the well-known story of the bishop who turned up at the front door of a convent, to be told, rather severely, to go round to the back. From the way he dressed, the nun at the door thought he was a tramp.

Two years ago, I bought myself a white tee-shirt. I was proud to wear it as one of the thousands of people who made a human chain round the centre of the city of Edinburgh, part of the Make Poverty History campaign. The fact that we all wore white did nothing to disguise our differences: we were short and tall, fat and thin, brown, black, yellow and white, young and old, of every political and religious persuasion. But we were totally united in this one thing: our passionate desire for the eradication of poverty.

Isaiah has a slightly different take on the image of clothing in this joyous hymn of praise:

> I will greatly rejoice in the LORD,
> my whole being shall exult in my God;
> for he has clothed me with the garments of salvation,
> he has covered me with the robe of righteousness.

Isaiah 61.10

* * *

Clothing 2

I tell you, do not worry about your life, what you will eat, or about your body, what you will wear.

Luke 12.22

Sadly, I do sometimes worry about what to wear, but not in the sense that I understand Jesus to mean. I believe he was concerned about those who might not have enough clothing to keep them warm, rather than those who wonder anxiously what to wear at a party. I don't consider myself a shopaholic or a victim of fashion, but I do spend an inordinate amount of time thinking about what to wear.

Why is this, and why are so many people like me? Of course, it's because we want people to think well of us. Appearances count for so much.

And yet I know, deep down, that it doesn't matter a whit what I wear. It's quite simply of no importance. Nor do my clothes tell anyone what I am really like.

We might ask, what did Jesus wear? Well, of course, we can't know, but it's a pretty safe guess that his appearance meant nothing to him, and he probably dressed in simple, practical garments no different from those of his disciples. So how is it that so many of our priests and bishops, representatives of Christ, must, at least on formal occasions, wear expensive, elaborate and often quite gorgeous robes? Jesus said, of the Pharisees, 'They do all their deeds to be seen by others; for they make their phylacteries broad and their fringes long' (Matthew 23.5).

The best advice I could give to anyone about clothing is 'Give it away!' There are people in our country who don't have enough clothes to keep them warm and safe from hypothermia. Most of these will be asylum seekers and refugees who don't have the money they need to live. And other people, not quite so destitute, can only afford to buy clothes at charity shops. God certainly does not want us to worry about what we wear, but I believe that he does want us to develop a sensitive attitude towards clothing in all its aspects, and towards everything that concerns us in our daily living.

* * *

Lost sheep

. . . go rather to the lost sheep of the house of Israel.
Matthew 10.6

Who are the lost sheep of today? Perhaps they are those people who have lost touch with the faith of their forebears. They may have deliberately walked away from organized religion, finding it completely irrelevant to their lives. They may have rejected the institutional nature of church, feeling uncomfortable with what they perceive to be narrow and outdated ideas. They may have grown up with little knowledge of God.

Nowadays in European countries, Christians are in a minority and sometimes despised as gullible and unthinking. They are the butts of jokes; they are frequently misunderstood. But when we consider our secular society, in what is sometimes called the 'post-Christian era', what do we see? We find that people of no faith nonetheless go in for worship and ritual too. Their 'gods' are different; they worship money, sporting heroes and especially 'celebrities', and they find comfort in rituals such as laying flowers in the place where someone has been killed.

We who are Christian (or members of any faith) have to beware of any smugness which leads us to think we are better than those who do not believe in God. We are not better, but we long to share the treasure that is our faith. Recently I heard of a priest who wanted to build a church with walls of glass so that people outside could look in and be attracted inside. But I believe that rather than trying to draw people in, we would be wiser to go out to meet them, to get to know them. Yes, their lives would be immeasurably enriched if they were drawn to God, but we should not underestimate how much the 'lost sheep' may have to give to us.

* * *

Empathy 1

Remember those who are in prison, as though you were in prison with them; those who are being tortured, as though you yourselves were being tortured.

Hebrews 13.3

The letter to the Hebrews is unlike all the other books in the New Testament. We don't know who its author was, but we do know it contains a good deal of wisdom and sound advice for the followers of Jesus.

The extract above is taken from a list of ways to live as Christians similar to those we read in St Paul's letters, promoting such values as mutual love, respect for marriage and hospitality.

But when I was reading through Chapter 13 I was particularly struck by the lines I have quoted.

Here the writer is making costly demands on his readers. As Christians we can't simply glide through life being nice to everybody. It is not enough to pray for people we know who are suffering, it is not even enough to visit them in hospices or in prisons. No, our concern for them has to run so deep that we are willing to share their pain and not only to give them compassion, which means suffering *with* them, but empathy, which means suffering *in* them – in other words, really coming to understand what it is like for them.

This is far from easy, not only because of the time it takes out of our lives, but also because often the gap in experience between the sufferer and the would-be consoler is just too wide to bridge. I vividly recall the sense of total inadequacy I felt the first time I went to try to comfort a friend whose husband had died less than an hour before.

However, in spite of the difficulties, I believe empathy is an ideal to aim for. It affects our prayer life too. I have a long list of people I pray for, and it's tempting to skim over each name with just a fleeting thought. I realize that I should give more time and more love.

* * *

Empathy 2

I thought, if another person knocks on the door,
I will scream.
They were all so kind,
so well-meaning and nice.
They brought me cakes
But I wasn't in the least bit hungry.
They brought me flowers
but I hadn't enough vases.
Some of them told me not to cry,
some of them told me to cry.

Some told me of their own experiences,
many said they would pray for me.
Some kissed and hugged me,
others seemed afraid to touch me.
They made me cups of tea,
endless, tasteless cups of tea.

Then Jill came.
She looked into my eyes
and sat down next to me.
I welcomed the silence
and the stillness of her.
I relaxed, and waited.
Nothing was said
till at last Jill spoke.
'It's hell, isn't it?' she said,
and I knew that she knew,
I understood that she understood.

* * *

Funerals

Precious in the sight of the LORD
is the death of his faithful ones.
                          Psalm 116.15

Sadly for me, my mother's funeral took place in a crematorium. Although we had filled in for the obliging clergyman some details of Mother's life, in the hopes of making the service less impersonal, I stood there feeling numb and thinking, 'I hate this.' The situation was redeemed for me by my mother's great-granddaughter, Arabella, then four years old.

Arabella's cat, Fred, had died the previous week. Suddenly the little girl spoke loud and clear into the solemn atmosphere: 'Mummy,' she said, 'I hope Fred doesn't jump up on Granny's lap in heaven, because Granny doesn't like cats very much.'

A few weeks after this our good friend Oliver died, dancing a circle dance with his friends. Some days later, on his seventy-second birthday, the family organized a service of celebration and thanksgiving.

Oliver was a profoundly spiritual man. The church was overflowing with people and flowers. There was an atmosphere of joy, beautiful music, prayer and silence. Oliver's three sons stood in the sanctuary and told us about him.

Oliver was greatly loved. He was exceptional in his talent as a painter, his depth as a thinker, exceptional in his gentleness and goodness. Of course, those who loved him will grieve. But they recognize that his life was a source of joy and the joy of Oliver lives on.

Oliver was 'special' and his funeral service was too. But even so, I can't help wishing it could be more like that for all of us. And sometimes, I like to think myself into the child's trust of Arabella and imagine them all among the angels and trumpets: Great-Granny, Oliver and Fred the cat.

May they rest in peace.

* * *

Outside 1

Jesus also suffered outside the city gate in order to sanctify the people by his own blood. Let us then go to him outside the camp and bear the abuse he endured.

Hebrews 13.12, 13

Here the writer of the letter to the Hebrews is asking us to be one with Jesus in his suffering, and Jesus himself is identified with those 'outside the camp'.

Sadly, in our day a great number of people have to live as outsiders. They are the ones who are excluded, for whatever reason, from the comfortable place of the majority. They are the ones who feel unaccepted, unwanted and unloved. They are the marginalized, or those 'off the page' altogether.

The list is long. It includes the poor, the unattractive, the unintelligent, the disabled and the addicted who live and work around us. It also includes people who impinge little on the day-to-day lives of those in the rich half of the world: the starving, the tortured, people with HIV/AIDS and children dying of dysentery.

As Christians, we don't really have a choice. We have to leave our comfort and pleasure behind in the camp and venture outside to meet others and invite them in. This can be more than uncomfortable: it can be threatening or humbling. But it will also be rewarding.

To be in solidarity with Jesus and all those 'outside the camp' is simply what Jesus requires, but unfortunately justice is not always a priority with churchgoers. All through the Gospels there is evidence of Christ's concern for the poor and the marginalized, and his wish that we should share this concern and take action accordingly.

Perhaps what we need most of all is increased awareness and sensitivity. Just to take one example, when we realize how many children die every day of malnutrition and disease, and try to stand in the shoes of their parents, then surely we will be moved to act.

* * *

Outside 2

Man of the Match

I went down to the Drop-In for refugees.
I didn't want to go.
I wanted to practise my bowling
and then have a drink with my mates.
But David, my brother, persuaded me.
I hated stepping inside that room,
not knowing what I would find,
not having the least idea what to do.

But I saw a lad of about my own age
standing outside the group,
so I went over to talk to him
thinking, if I feel awkward,
what must it be like for him?
It was he, Ali, who put me at my ease.
His English was excellent,
better than mine, I daresay.
I wouldn't have thought of mentioning cricket,
but Ali asked if I played.
It wasn't long before I invited him home,
and now he's in the team.
He's a bowler, like me,
but better by far.
He lives with his mum on a council estate,
he has no money,
he's not allowed to work,
he's waiting for permission to stay.
And last week, when we won
for the first time this season,
Ali was named Man of the Match.

* * *

Innocence

Truly I tell you, unless you change and become like children,
you will never enter the kingdom of heaven.

Matthew 18.3

Our small village had a pub, a church, a school and a post office.
It also happened to have a teenage boy who might at one time
have been dubbed 'the village idiot'. Johnny couldn't speak or
walk properly, and it was impossible to know how much he
understood, but he was a cheery soul who laughed a lot. We
were all fond of him.

However, I wouldn't have chosen to live with Johnny. Jean
Vanier, on the other hand, has devoted his life to living with

and looking after people with mental disabilities. He founded L'Arche, an international organization which sets up homes for people with severe learning difficulties, homes where they can live alongside people who don't have their problems. Jean isn't just fond of his companions; he loves them deeply and dearly.

People with acute learning difficulties have the same lovely quality as very young children, of being true to themselves and so to others, of being transparent and real. The rest of us, the so-called normal and grown up, have for the most part succeeded in hiding our real selves from view. We present others with a façade that we hope will make them like us, approve of us, admire us. And often we become so skilled at constructing this camouflage that we ourselves lose sight of our own truth.

I might ask myself: 'What is the truth about me? Can I peel away these layers of sham and instead become transparent to others? Can I become like a little child or an innocent person?'

God knows each one of us. He sees through all our pretences and, wonderfully, he loves us just as we are, however false or flawed or fragile.

And in response to such love I hope I can begin to unlearn everything that is not real in me, and show my true self to the people in my life, becoming innocent again.

* * *

Holidays 1

He said to them, 'Come away to a deserted place all by your-selves and rest a while.'

Mark 6.31

Did Jesus ever take a holiday? It seems unlikely. On this occasion he took the disciples with him and they sailed to a lonely spot hoping for a break from the crowds. The strategy failed, because the crowds followed him there, and he took pity on them and began to teach them.

We also know that Jesus sometimes escaped by himself to the hills, but that was hardly a holiday: it was to give himself time to pray, to be alone with his Father.

It is very different for me. I live in a place where other people come for their holidays. I am near the sea and beautiful countryside. Yet I am very much looking forward to my next holiday, which promises to give me so many things to enjoy: boats and islands, a place I have never visited before, a lot of interesting history and the company of good friends. But even while I eagerly anticipate these days away, I ask myself: do I really need a holiday?

I hope it will enrich my experience, that I will learn something new, that it will be fun. I also think it will be good to leave behind for a while the commitments and pressures of my daily life. But I wonder, shouldn't I perhaps be content now, towards the end of my life, to enjoy what I have here, to 'bloom where I am planted', to make the most of my own place?

There are many people who cannot afford a holiday at all. I wonder if there isn't a kind of greed in seeking more and more experiences, spending more and more money in the quest for excitement and adventure. I don't want to become a stay-at-home stick-in-the-mud, but I think it would take a lifetime to explore all the possibilities of being right here.

* * *

Holidays 2

Megan had saved up for a long time to go on safari in Kenya. She had a wonderful time; the wild animals she saw were even more magnificent and impressive than she had been led to believe.

To her surprise, at the end of the safari she still had time and money to spare, so she decided to spend both in Nairobi. The glossy brochure she had been given described the city as having a population of two million, so it was something of a shock to discover that it contained the world's largest slum, home to three million of the very poor.

Megan, against the advice of friends, went to see the slum for herself and was horrified at the plight of the people struggling to exist there. The conditions under which they had to live were filthy and degrading, and for Megan the only redeeming feature of the place was the presence of the Salvation Army, whose officers actually lived among the people.

She couldn't get this place out of her mind. Back at her luxurious hotel she had a shower and then went down to sit by the swimming pool. The contrast between her surroundings and what she had seen that day unnerved her. She didn't swim or speak with any of the other guests, and after a while a smiling waiter came up and asked her if she would like anything to eat. Megan wasn't hungry, but she ordered a small snack and when the waiter came back she asked him if he would mind answering some questions.

He readily agreed, and showed no resentment when she asked how much he earned in a day. When he answered her question she realized that his wage was far less than the cost of her snack. She was not surprised when this clean, courteous young man told her where he lived, and she knew that in Nairobi's notorious slum he would often go hungry.

* * *

A wonder-filled day

My soul, give thanks to the LORD,
all my being, bless his holy name.
Psalm 103.1, Grail Psalms

I feel my heart overflowing with thankfulness. This day was blessed, as all our days are blessed, but in a special way:

through an encounter with two old friends, and with the heart-wrenching loveliness of spring just coming into its own.

I had not seen either of my friends for 20 years. First we met Stuart. He is well off, successful and in the best of health. We don't share the same beliefs in the fundamentals of politics or religion, but our friendship needed no re-kindling. Stuart is a very busy man, but he gladly makes regular visits to an old lady, no relation of his, who is suffering from dementia. He made time for us today.

The second friend is a priest I will call Bernard. He has chosen to share his house with strangers: a homeless man and a family with nowhere to live. Bernard is in constant pain, but he says, 'Life is fun.' He loves his home, his friends, his neighbours and his church. He spends time with prostitutes, drug addicts and the wealthy traditionalists in his parish. Today he too made time for us.

The sun shone all day and there was blossom everywhere. Trees seemed to open their leaves as we watched. I stood and looked up at the tall copper beech, radiant in its first glory. I looked down at clumps of primroses and violets, and the sheets of white and blue windflowers. There was such a wealth of beauty on this April afternoon.

So after such a day, I certainly feel that 'my cup runneth over' (Psalm 23, Authorized Version).

* * *

Remembering

Blessed are those who mourn, for they will be comforted.
Matthew 5.4

We climbed to the church
on top of the cliff
to remember Mairi,
[as though we could forget her
who lived, a bright spirit, among us].

104

We, her friends, oddly diverse,
a ragbag of mourners:
young and old,
sceptics and devout,
proper and harum-scarum
but alike in grief,
united in heavy-heartedness.

The ancient church was cold but peaceful.
There were lilies, her favourite flower,
and candles for us to light.
We spoke or were silent,
we listened or prayed.

I think it must have been love
that drew us together then,
and I thought how Mairi would have smiled
to see that assorted jumble of her friends
gathered to honour her
in the name of Jesus.

* * *

Awakening

Then God said, 'Let there be light,' and there was light.

Genesis 1.3

Hafiz, the celebrated Persian poet of the fourteenth century,
wrote:

Even after all this time,
the sun never says to the earth,
'You owe me.'
Look what happens with a love like that:
It lights the whole sky.

The Gift: Poems by Hafiz the Great Sufi
Master, translated by Daniel Ladinsky
(Penguin Books Australia, 1999)

We take them for granted: the sunshine and God.
We wake every morning to a new day,
to a world full of light and a love
that is new every morning.
We don't stop to notice or wonder,
and rarely pause to give thanks to our God
for the sunshine and all of creation.
We take them for granted: our sight and our hearing,
our smelling and tasting and touching.
We live half-blind, half-deaf, half-dumb
tight closed like buds that fail to open.
There is a world of waiting,
a world of light and loveliness
waiting for us to flower.
And God waits too, for our response,
our invitation, our embrace,
for our awakening.

* * *

Possession

*Do not be afraid, little flock, for it is your Father's good
pleasure to give you the kingdom. Sell your possessions, and
give alms . . . For where your treasure is, there your heart will
be also.*

Luke 12.32–34

Salomon, a young Christian friend, was forced to flee from Zaz,
a tiny village somewhere in 'the back of beyond' between the
Tigris and the Euphrates. Speaking very courteously, he said to
me once, 'The difference between you people in the west and
us is that you are concerned about *having* and we are concerned
about *being*.'

We have only to think about our present craze for shopping
and consumerism to know that he is right. Possessions mean
a great deal to most of us in western countries.

Buddhists believe in *metta*, a love which is without the desire to possess, but only to be of help to others. It is good to ask ourselves: 'Do I really need this or that thing?' The answer is usually no. To me, the most beautiful places of worship are the ones that are uncluttered by artefacts. In Assisi, the Basilica is unquestionably marvellous, but a place that speaks of God more powerfully to me is the lesser known medieval church of St Stefano, its walls unadorned as in the days of Francis.

Blessed are the poor in spirit, and who are they? I guess they are the ones who are *pure* in spirit, who see no necessity to own anything beyond the essentials of living. They find joy and fulfilment not in possessing, but in receiving whatever comes their way with humility and gratitude, be it rain or sunshine, tears or laughter, sickness or pain or dementia, or gifts which are the expression of the love of friends.

* * *

Newness of life

Cast away from you all the transgressions that you have committed against me, and get yourselves a new heart and a new spirit.

Ezekiel 18.31

A very long time ago, when I was a little girl, there was a craze for having autograph books. These had sturdy hardback covers and each page was a different pastel colour.

Celebrities were an unknown species in those days, and at my end of the small town where I grew up, nobody knew anyone famous, so the pages of our autograph books were filled with verses and good wishes from our relations, friends and classmates.

In my mind's eye, I can still see the pale green page where Janice chose to write:

New friends are like silver,
Old friends are like gold.

Well, the autograph book was lost in my childhood, but Janice is still alive, and still a good friend. I am not particularly interested in precious metals, or knowledgeable about the relative merits of silver and gold, but I am convinced that it is pointless to make comparisons between old friends and new. Both are of great value to me.

I love to spend time with Janice and other long-standing friends of my own age, especially when we reminisce about the old days and laugh at the old jokes and remember the good times. But equally I rejoice in my new friends of whatever age, because they open my mind to fresh ways of thinking and share their different stories and experiences with me. I think of my new young neighbours, John and Lily, and the joy they bring into our lives simply by being who they are.

I thank God for the enrichment that friends old and new have brought me.

* * *

A bad name

When he arrived at the Pharisee's house and took his place at table, a woman came in, who had a bad name in the town.
Luke 7.36–37, Jerusalem Bible

Francis, Michael and Gus were Little Brothers of Jesus. They went to live in social housing on a sink estate where their mission was to live no differently from the neighbours around them, never preaching but offering their friendship and hospitality and help where they could. Francis got a job as a cleaner in the local hospital and Michael found work as a garage hand, but Gus, who was quite a lot older, was unemployed.

The neighbours were not slow to accept them and it didn't take long for them to be on speaking terms with almost everyone. There was one person on their own street, however, an elderly widow called Patsy, who had a bad name on the estate, and 'the boys', as people called them, could make no headway in getting to know her. Their smiles were met with ferocious glares, and when Gus plucked up the courage to call round and see her one day, she opened the door, let out a stream of swear words and then slammed it in his face.

One cold night they were trudging home after a long stint at the local drop-in centre. A blizzard was blowing in their faces as they climbed the steep road to the estate. Francis was hungry. 'What's for supper, Gus?' he asked. Gus stopped dead in his tracks. 'Oh no!' he said, 'Mike, Frank, I'm so sorry. I forgot it was my turn.'

When they got into the house and looked in the fridge, there was nothing except a small plate of cold mashed potatoes. They were staring at it dolefully, struggling to be cheerful and positive, when the doorbell rang.

To their surprise, Patsy stood on the doorstep, arms akimbo as usual.

'I wondered if you boys was hungry,' she said. 'I've made a big hotpot and a nice rice pudding if you'd like to come round and eat it. I got you all wrong, see. I've been watching you, and I seen you helping a lot of folks. And you got no airs and graces, like some. So come on over, lads.'

* * *

His brother's keeper

Then the LORD said to Cain, 'Where is your brother Abel?' He said, 'I do not know. Am I my brother's keeper?'

Genesis 4.9

Our ten-year-old grandson has been staying with us for a week.

One afternoon we sat on either side of the fire enjoying a conversation. I did most of the talking, because what he wanted to hear was stories, especially true stories about his father as a small boy. The best stories, of course, were the ones about when his father was naughty.

Damian is a quiet child, and an eager listener. I liked watching his face as I talked. When I had exhausted my reminiscences of 'Daddy', he asked after another friend, Frank.

I know Frank very well indeed. Damian has only met him once or twice, but for some reason this young man, who has a lot of problems, interested him.

I told Damian what I knew of Frank. I told him the story of something that happened to Frank quite recently, a sad story with a happy ending.

As I was finishing the account I saw Damian's face change. He looked at me with an expression of such gladness and relief that I almost stopped in mid-sentence.

What struck me was that he should be so moved by someone else's fate. I realized, with a kind of awe, that somewhere along the line, young Damian has learnt to be his brother's keeper.

* * *

Wonder

> *I thank you for the wonder of my being.*
> Psalm 139.14, Grail Psalms

Psalm 139 is in itself reflective and is also full of material for us to use in reflection. It is about God and about ourselves in relation to him. At first sight, the line quoted above may shock us, as it seems so self-congratulatory and the very opposite of humble. But it expresses true, as distinct from false, humility, because it is the wonderfulness of God that has made us what we are. Another translation puts it differently: 'I praise you, for I am wonderfully made.'

The psalm is above all a song of adoration and confidence in God.

> I thank you for the wonder of my being,
> that I can breathe and run and dance and sing,
> that I can wonder.

110

I wonder at the freshness of early morning,
the renewal of spring,
the consolation of an embrace,
the happiness of laughter shared.
I wonder at man's inventions,
marvellous and terrible.
I wonder at the suffering and pain
that devastates creation
and hurts the innocent;
at the endurance of the human spirit.

I wonder, and I thank you for your promise
given in love,
faithful, everlasting, universal,
the only hope:
'I will be with you till the end of time.'

* * *

Magic

> . . . *you make the clouds your chariot,*
> *you ride on the wings of the wind.*
> Psalm 104.3

Gerard Manley Hopkins wrote a poem which begins: 'Glory be to God for dappled things'. God, who rides on the wings of the wind, also made things which are 'beyond', which are 'original, spare, strange', and which are surely 'magical'.

One such is the waterfall our friend showed us last week. It plunges from a great height into a remote and secret valley. The little beck races down the bank, sparkling in the sunshine. It hits the narrow space between a hard place and a rock, stumbles for a second in a froth of silvery bubbles, then tumbles head-long over the edge and down the precipice which the bank has now become: a fall of living water.

Then today, I saw another natural, magical phenomenon in Shetland.

> There it lies,
> a slender strip of creamy sand,
> walkway to a small green isle
> where Ninian's chapel stood:
> the tombolo.
> On either side the rounded curve
> of bluey-green sea water laps
> softly and steadily against the bar.
> Beyond, the black rocks stride the bay,
> jagged and broken, fantastically shaped,
> yet guarding, sheltering, safekeeping
> this rare created thing,
> the tombolo.

Glory be to God for magical things.

* * *

Marvels

> *O sing to the LORD a new song,*
> *for he has done marvellous things.*
>   Psalm 98.1

> On Orkney, we went to Skara Brae,
> a village built five thousand years ago,
> before the Pyramids or the Great Wall of China,
> long before Jesus.
> We stared in wonder at the ancient houses
> and thought of those who lived there once,
> and died, leaving no weapons,
> a peace-loving people.
> We stared and wondered and thought,
> this is a treasure,

a tribute to the ingenuity
of humankind.

But walking away
I looked at the sunlit sea.
I listened to the steady sighing of the waves
and heard the calling of the oystercatcher.
I thought, were not these here,
the sea, the birds
and a sky like this
fifty thousand years ago?
And I wondered at the marvellous ways of God.

* * *

Belief

God is love, and those who abide in love abide in God, and God abides in them.

1 John 4.16

What is God really like?

To the Jews of the Old Testament he was all-powerful, capable of vengeance and what we would nowadays consider to be appalling cruelty. To most present-day Christians he is abounding in love and mercy, awesome and almighty yet intimately tender with his children.

But no-one has all the answers. We cannot tidy God away in a labelled box, for his Holy Spirit is forever free. Surely each of us can only believe in him as we experience him.

The God I personally believe in is all-loving, yes, but not all-powerful. It seems to me that there is an insidious thread running through the weft of our world, causing suffering and disfiguring creation.

Millions of us have watched David Attenborough's remarkable films, which show us the beauty of the earth but also occasionally bring us face to face with the sheer cruelty of Nature 'red in tooth and claw'. I have known people who have rejected God altogether after seeing such manifestations of savagery. I cannot see the hand of God in any violent act, but I do see him in the sensitivity and compassion of the very people who cry out against cruelty in all its forms.

The God I believe in is love. But to answer my own question, 'What is God really like?', we cannot know, not yet.

* * *

For the love of God

Each of you must give as you have made up your mind, not reluctantly or under compulsion, for God loves a cheerful giver.
2 Corinthians 9.7

Francis had been vicar of his inner-city parish for 40 years and a widower for 17 of them. He had always been hard-working, and spent most of his time cycling to visit the elderly and housebound. He was somewhat scatterbrained and disorganized, and so lacking in self-interest that he failed to remember that his seventieth birthday was imminent.

However, his parishioners had somehow discovered this and organized a collection. It was a poor parish, but the people responded willingly and with generosity for a man they respected and, in many cases, loved. To his astonishment, in the evening of his birthday (which he still had not remembered), Francis was presented with £500 in cash.

Afterwards, still feeling stunned, he sat in his study holding a wad of £50 notes. He began to think of ways to spend it. He had always longed to go to Assisi; perhaps he could afford it now. Or he could buy a new bicycle or perhaps do something about his garden. He had no idea of what any of these things would cost but he was aware of a pleasing sense of excitement.

After a while he pulled himself together. He must tidy his office and sort out his correspondence before he went to bed. Among a mass of papers on his desk, his eye fell on the local paper. He picked it up and began to read about a family unknown to him personally. They were hoping to raise enough money to take their seriously ill daughter to America for an operation which just might save her life. Francis hesitated for perhaps 30 seconds. Then he placed his £500 in a stout envelope and sealed it firmly. Next morning he arranged to have it delivered to the family, anonymously.

It was not at all what his parishioners had in mind for him, but if they had discovered what he had done, they would not have been surprised, because he did it for the love of God.

The Society for Promoting Christian Knowledge (SPCK) was founded in 1698. Its mission statement is:

To promote Christian knowledge by

- **Communicating the Christian faith in its rich diversity;**
- **Helping people to understand the Christian faith and to develop their personal faith; and**
- **Equipping Christians for mission and ministry.**

SPCK Worldwide serves the Church through Christian literature and communication projects in over 100 countries, and provides books for those training for ministry in many parts of the developing world. This worldwide service depends upon the generosity of others and all gifts are spent wholly on ministry programmes, without deductions.

SPCK Bookshops support the life of the Christian community by making available a full range of Christian literature and other resources, providing support for those training for ministry, and assisting bookstalls and book agents throughout the UK.

SPCK Publishing produces Christian books and resources, covering a wide range of inspirational, pastoral, practical and academic subjects. Authors are drawn from many different Christian traditions, and publications aim to meet the needs of a wide variety of readers in the UK and throughout the world.

The Society does not necessarily endorse the individual views contained in its publications, but hopes they stimulate readers to think about and further develop their Christian faith.

For further information about the Society, visit our website at *www.spck.org.uk* or write to:
SPCK, 36 Causton Street,
London SW1P 4ST, United Kingdom.